Fahd Burki *Works from 2003–2013*

Fahd Burki

Works from 2003–2013

SKIRA

Cover
Untitled
Acrylics and marker
on paper
47.5 x 38 cm
2012
Collection of John Dodelande

Editor
Rosa Maria Falvo

Editorial coordination
Eva Vanzella

Copy editor
Emanuela Di Lallo

Layout
Barbara Galotta

Photography
Faheem Ahmad
Jahanzeb Burki
Maciej Urbanek
Musthafa Aboobacker
Shahzeb Bhatti

Design
Dana Jamal

First published in Italy in 2014
by Skira Editore S.p.A.
Palazzo Casati Stampa
via Torino 61
20123 Milano
Italy
www.skira.net

Printed and bound in Italy. First edition

ISBN 978-88-572-2228-8 (Skira)
978-88-572-2362-9 (Grey Noise)

Distributed in USA, Canada,
Central & South America
by Rizzoli International Publications,
Inc., 300 Park Avenue South, New York,
NY 10010, USA.
Distributed elsewhere in the world
by Thames and Hudson Ltd., 181A
High Holborn, London WC1V 7QX,
United Kingdom.

Contents

Foreword

Grey Noise is pleased to present *Fahd Burki Works from 2003–2013*, the first in a series of artist monographs published in collaboration with Milan's Skira editore. The series marks an important expansion of our innovative exhibition programme beyond the physical limits of our gallery's walls.

Over the past decade Lahore-based Fahd Burki has set himself apart from his peers through his wholly unique and idiosyncratic visual language, and his thoughtful engagement with and serious investment in the practice of painting. Through the years our conviction in and commitment to his work has only strengthened and we are proud to share his achievements in this book.

We would like to thank the collectors who have supported Fahd since we first exhibited his work, and the writers and curators who have reflected on and helped initiate the growing critical dialogue about his art practice. Particular thanks go out to Murtaza Vali, who contributed the essay included in this book, and Rosa Maria Falvo for her encouragement and advice.

Finally, our deepest gratitude goes out to the two people without whom this book would not have been possible, Fahd Burki and Jean Marc Decrop.

Umer Butt and Hetal Pawani
Directors, Grey Noise

Robot
Oil on canvas
122 x 107 cm
2003

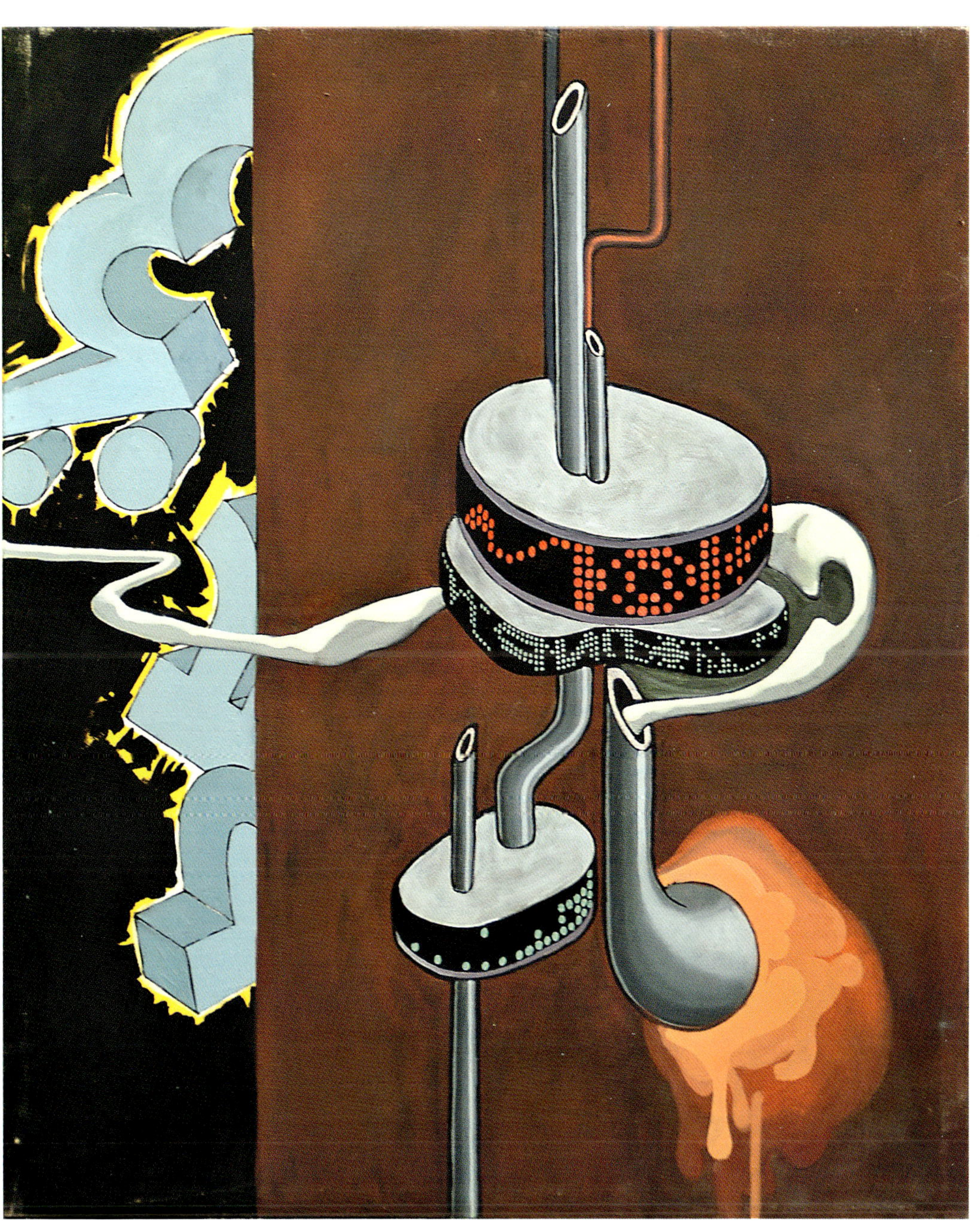

Vespa
Oil on canvas
107 x 122 cm
2003

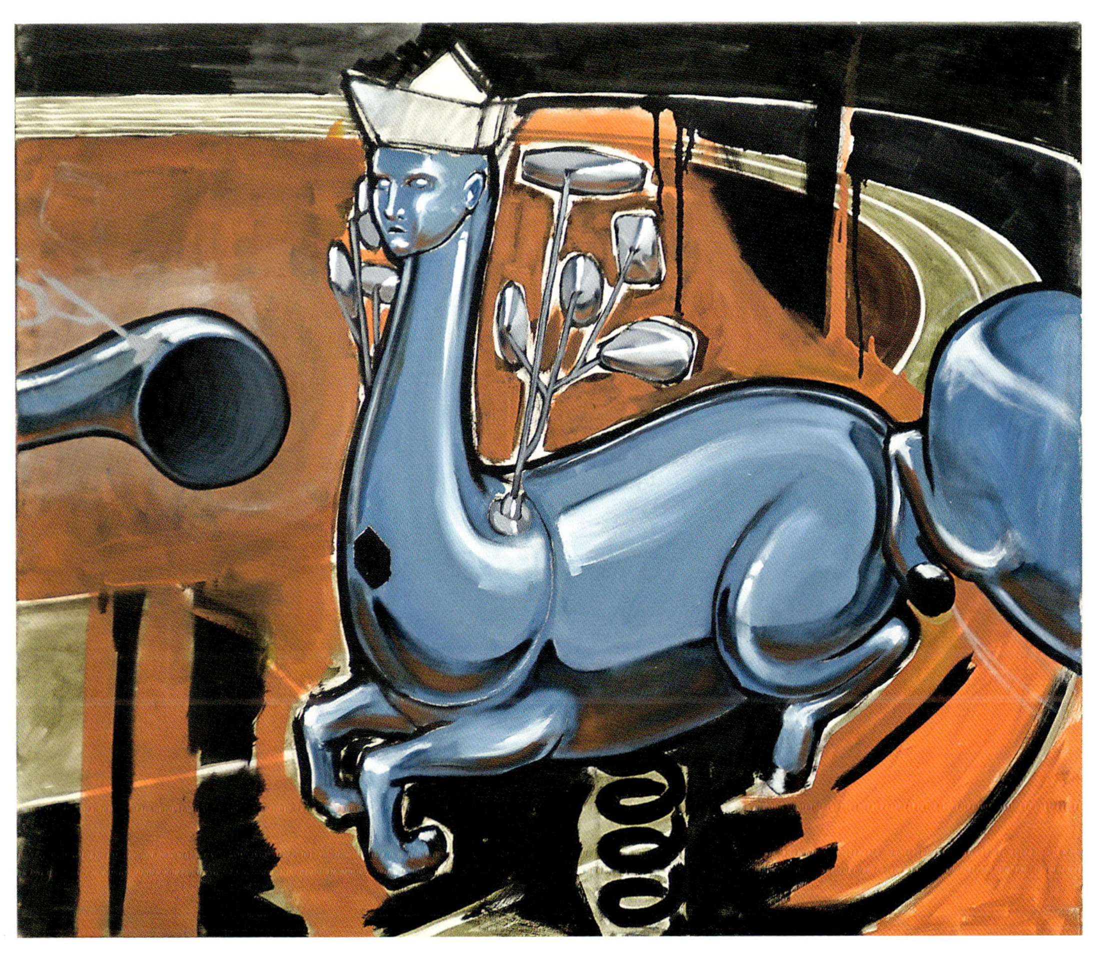

Untitled
Oil on canvas
165 x 137 cm
2004

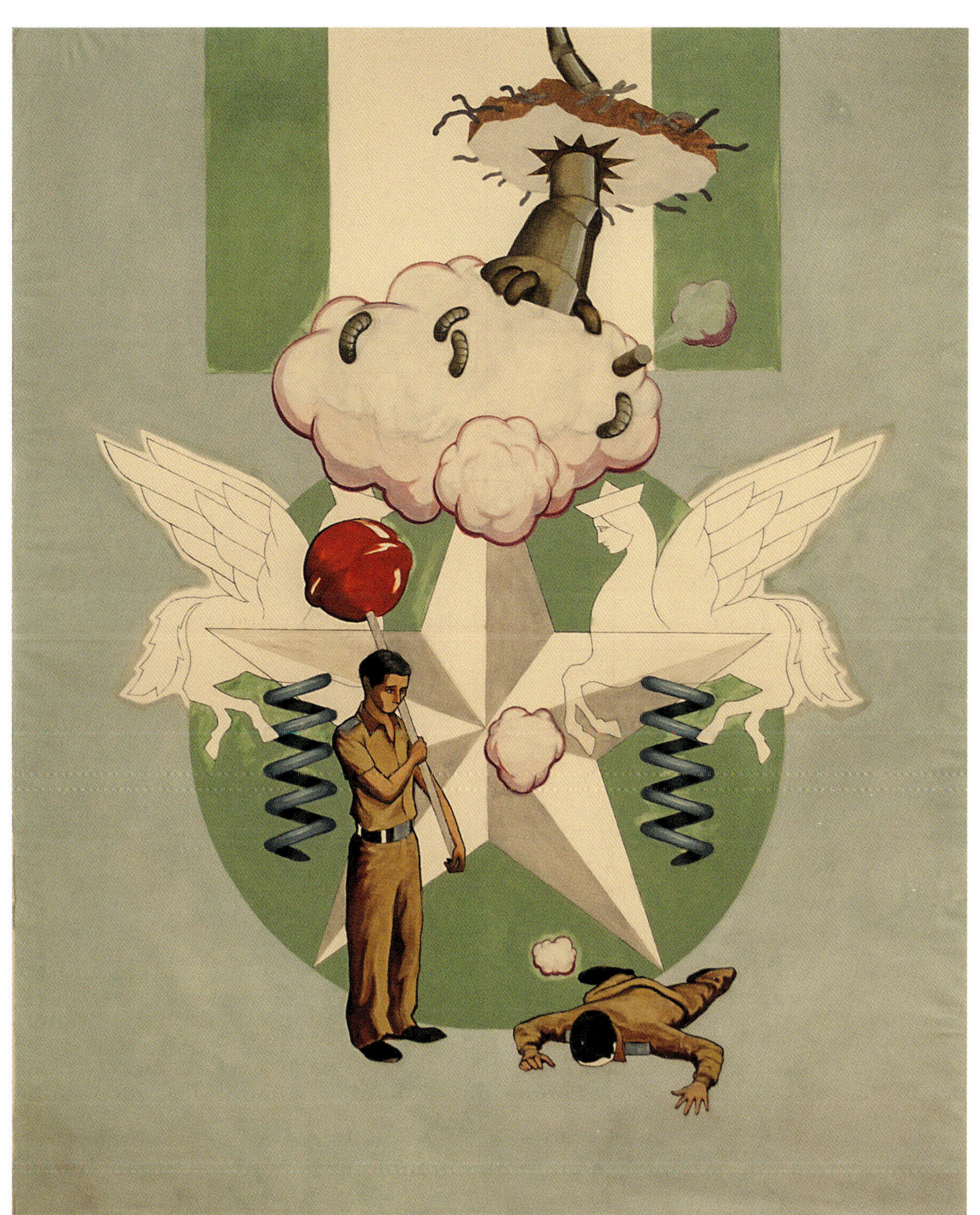

Untitled
Oil on canvas
196 x 161 cm
2004

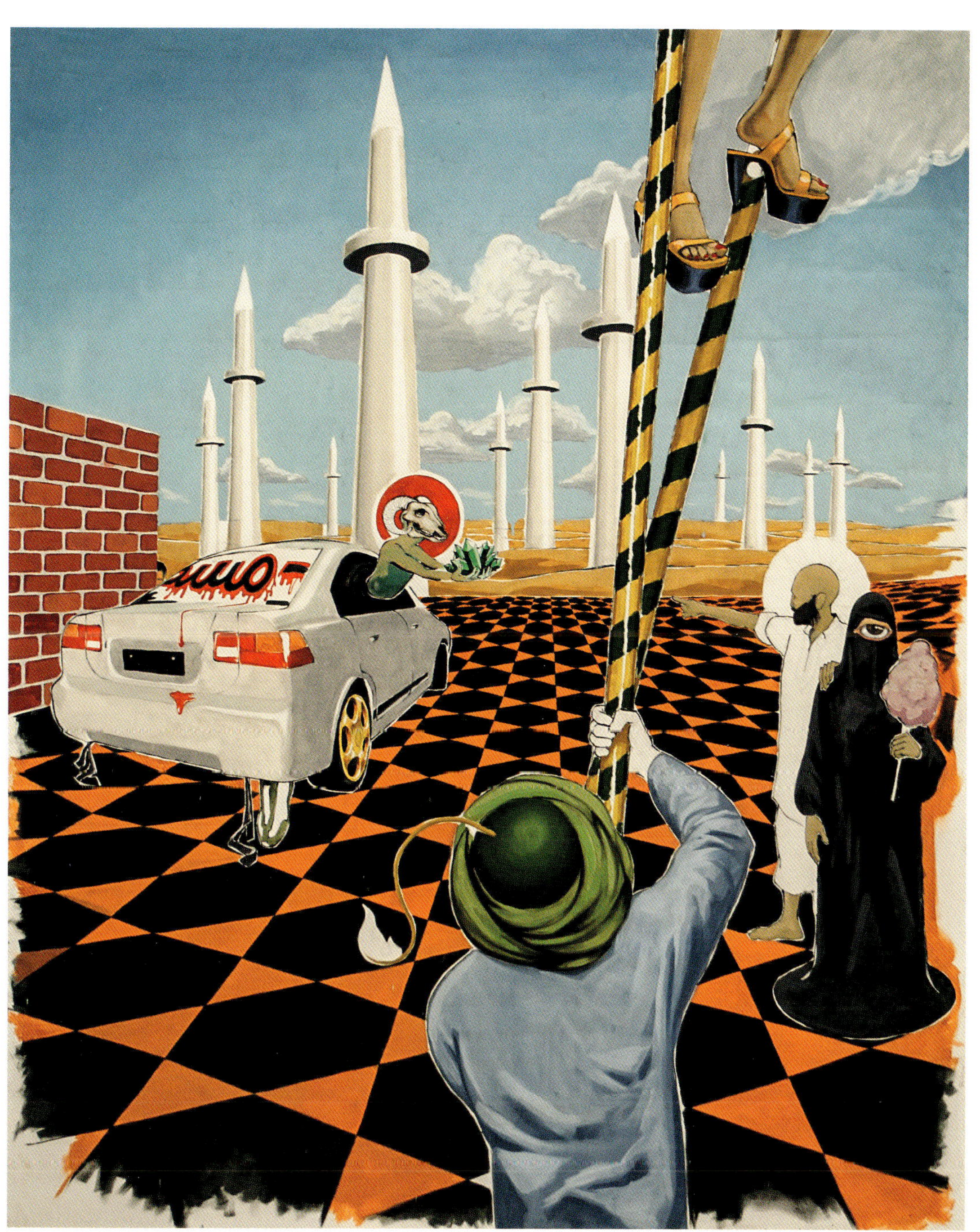

3arajo

Whisperer
Oil on canvas
152 x 122 cm
2004

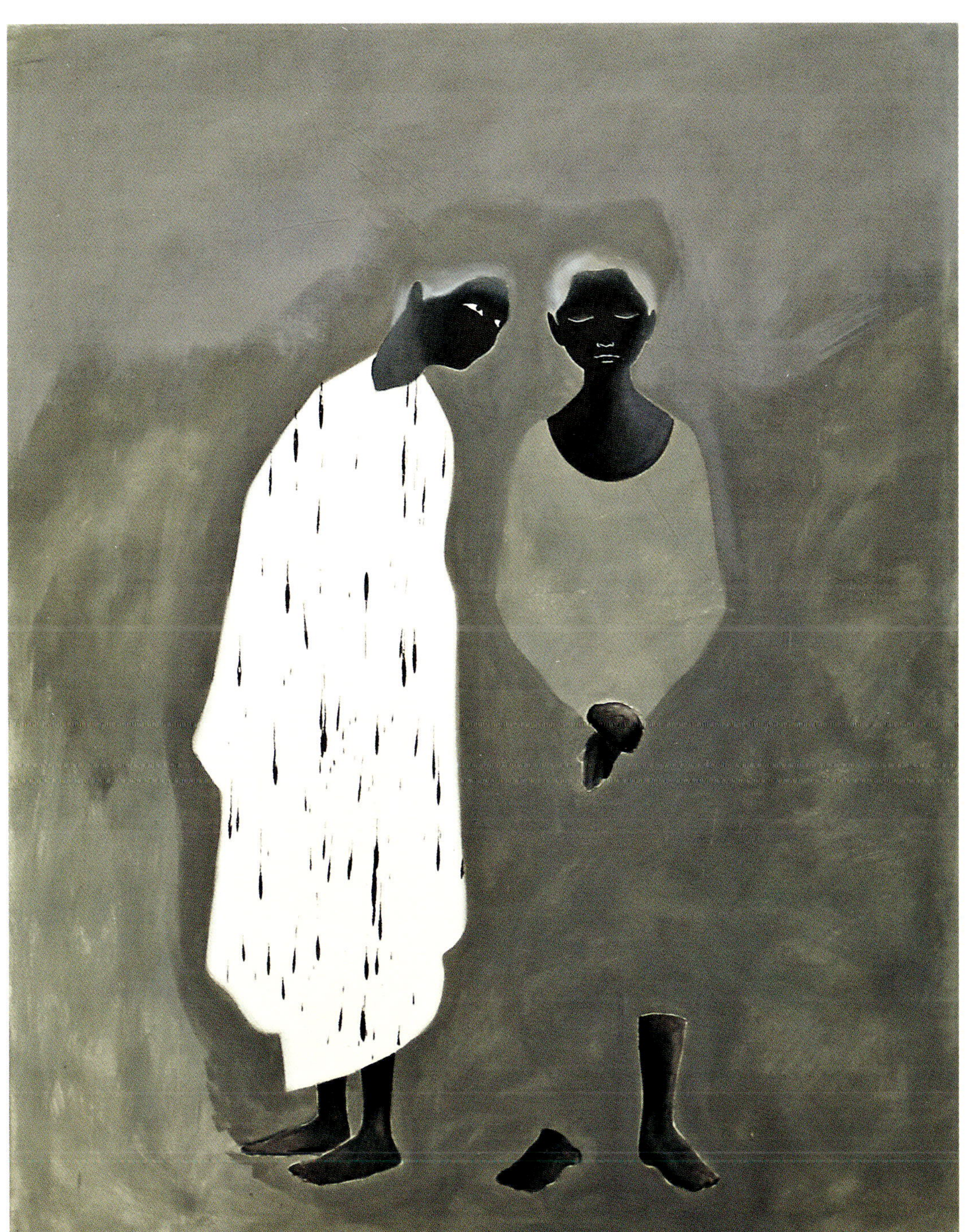

City
Oil on canvas
213 x 168 cm
2005

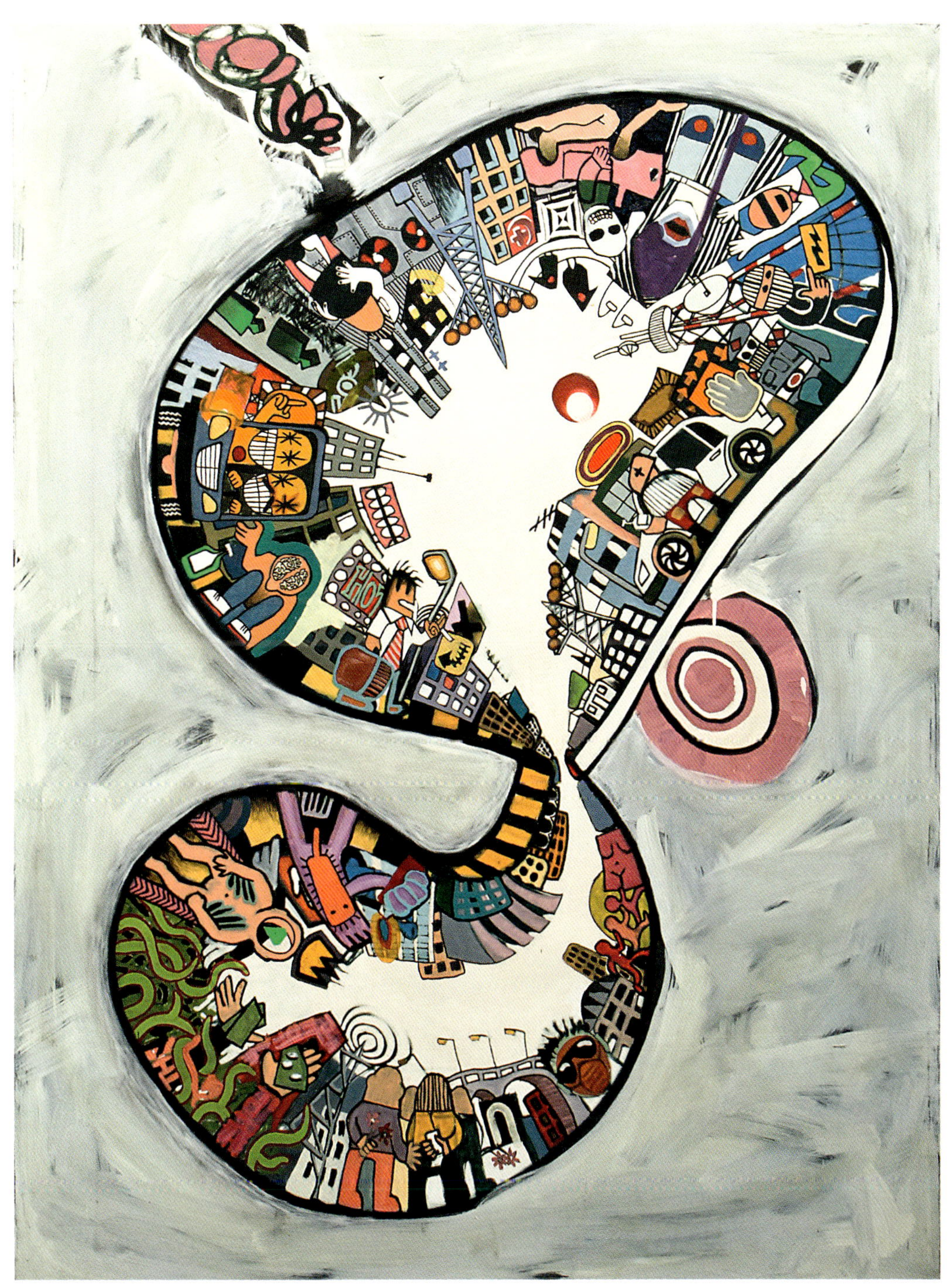

Untitled
(with Characters)
Oil on canvas
168 x 213 cm
2005

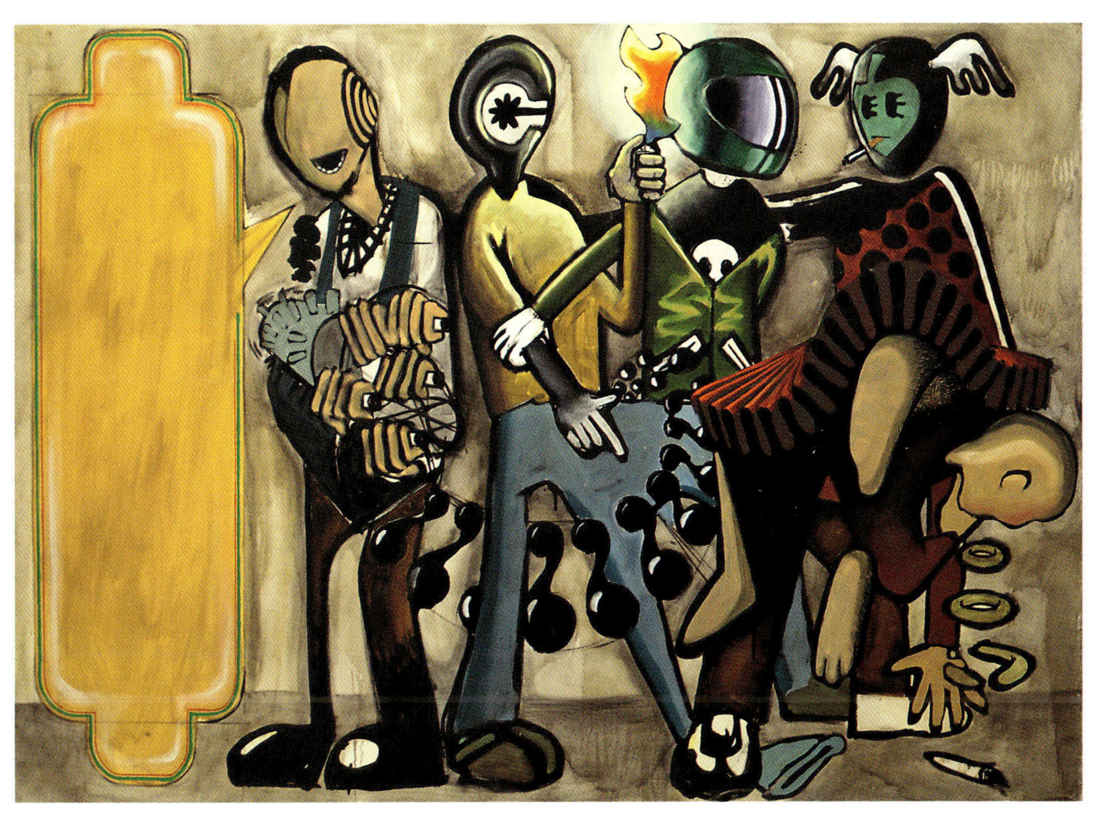

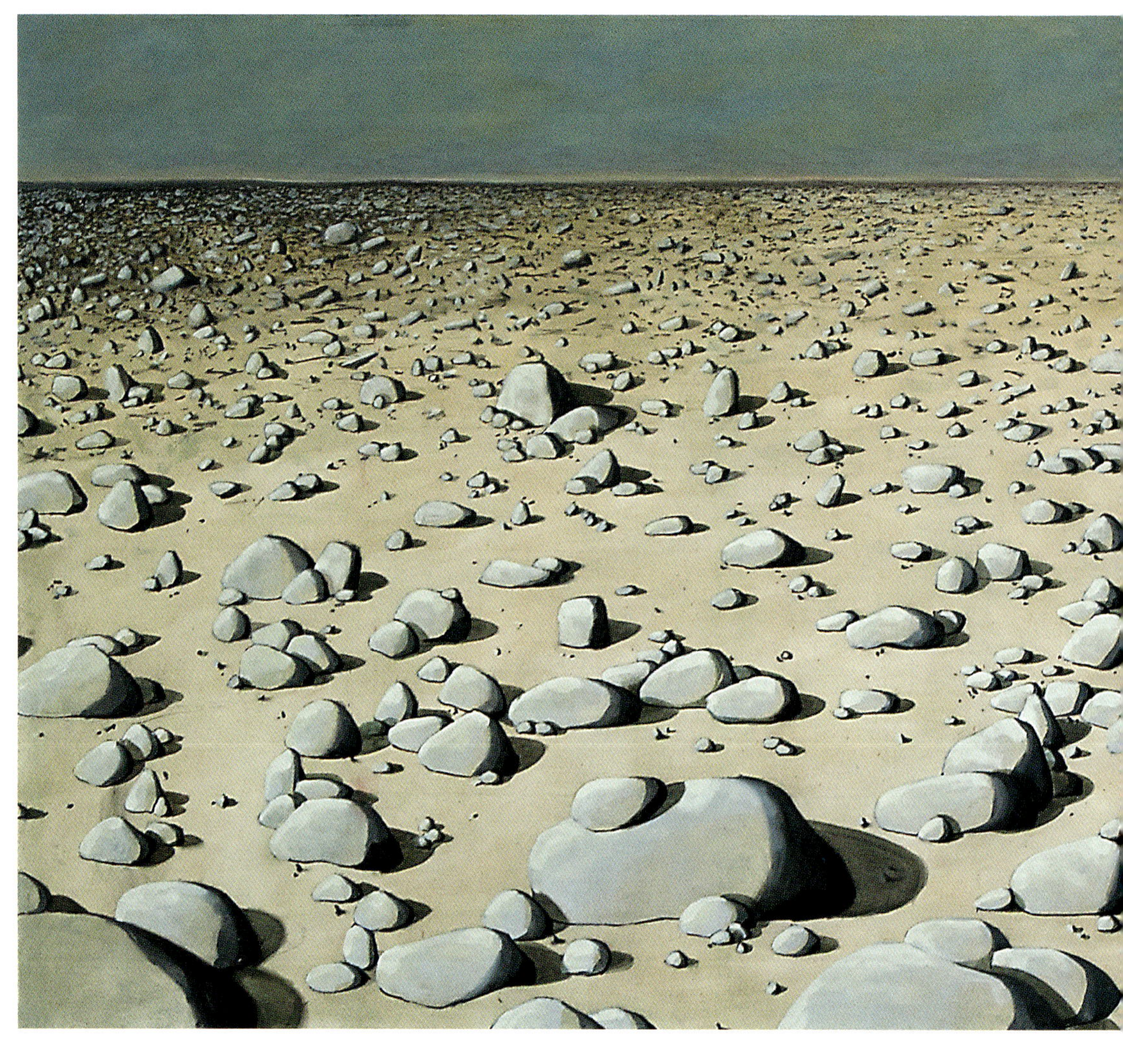

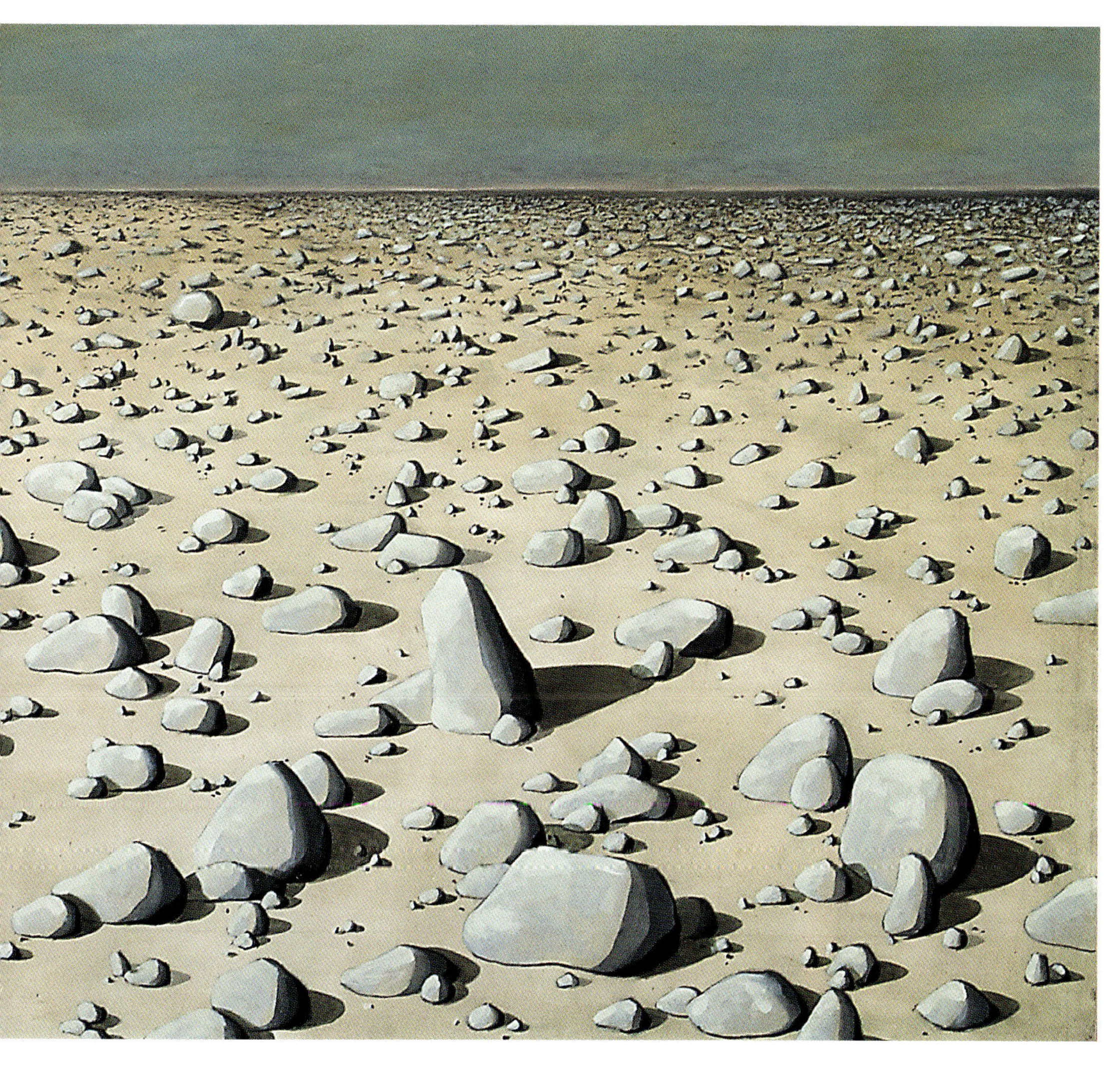

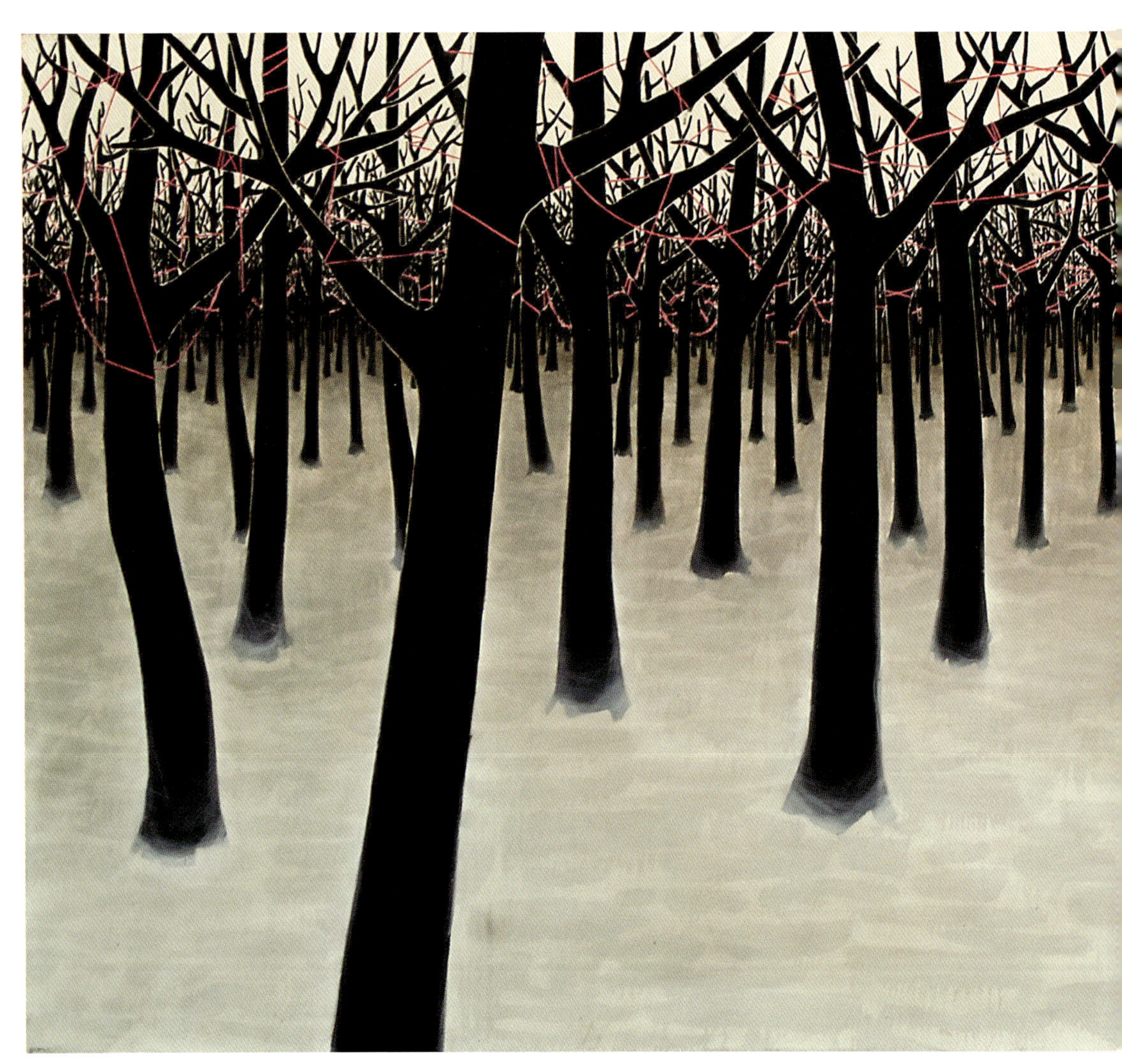

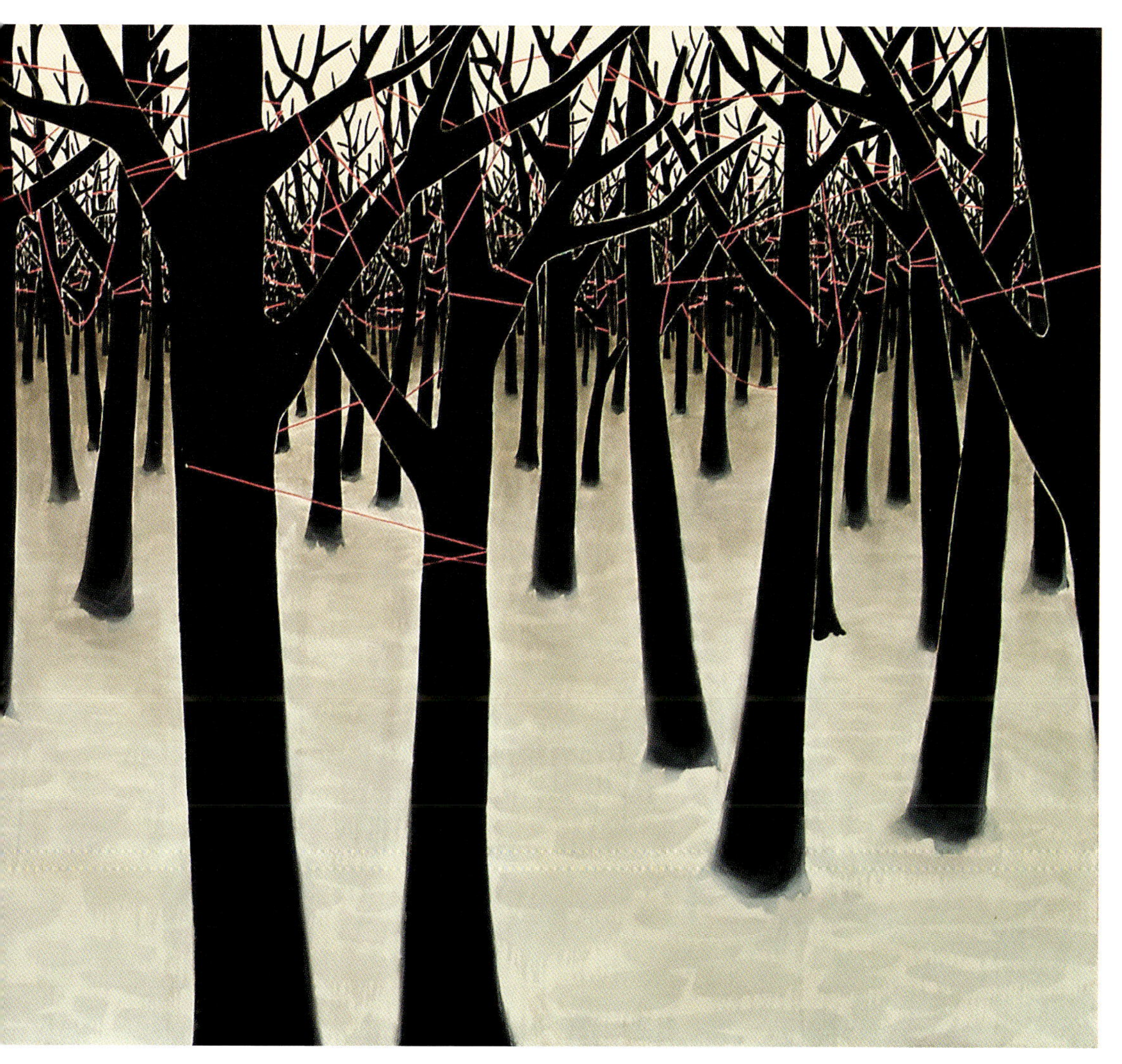

Pages 24–25
Tract 1
Oil on canvas
168 x 366 cm
2006

Pages 26–27
Tract 2
Oil on canvas
168 x 366 cm
2006

Right
Untitled (dog)
Acrylics on paper
40 x 30 cm
2007

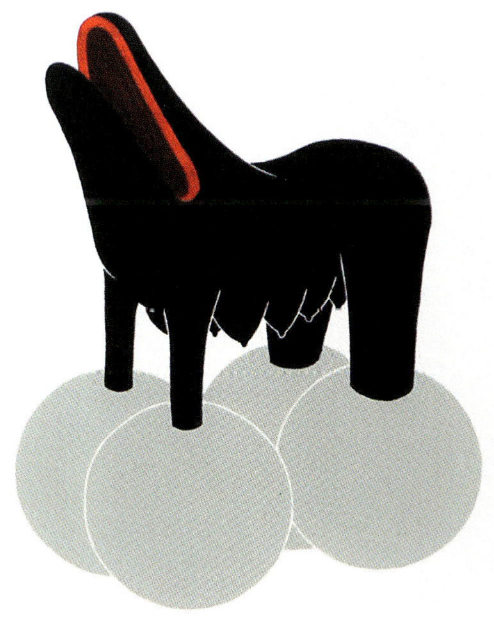

Revelers
Acrylics on paper
40 x 30 cm
2007

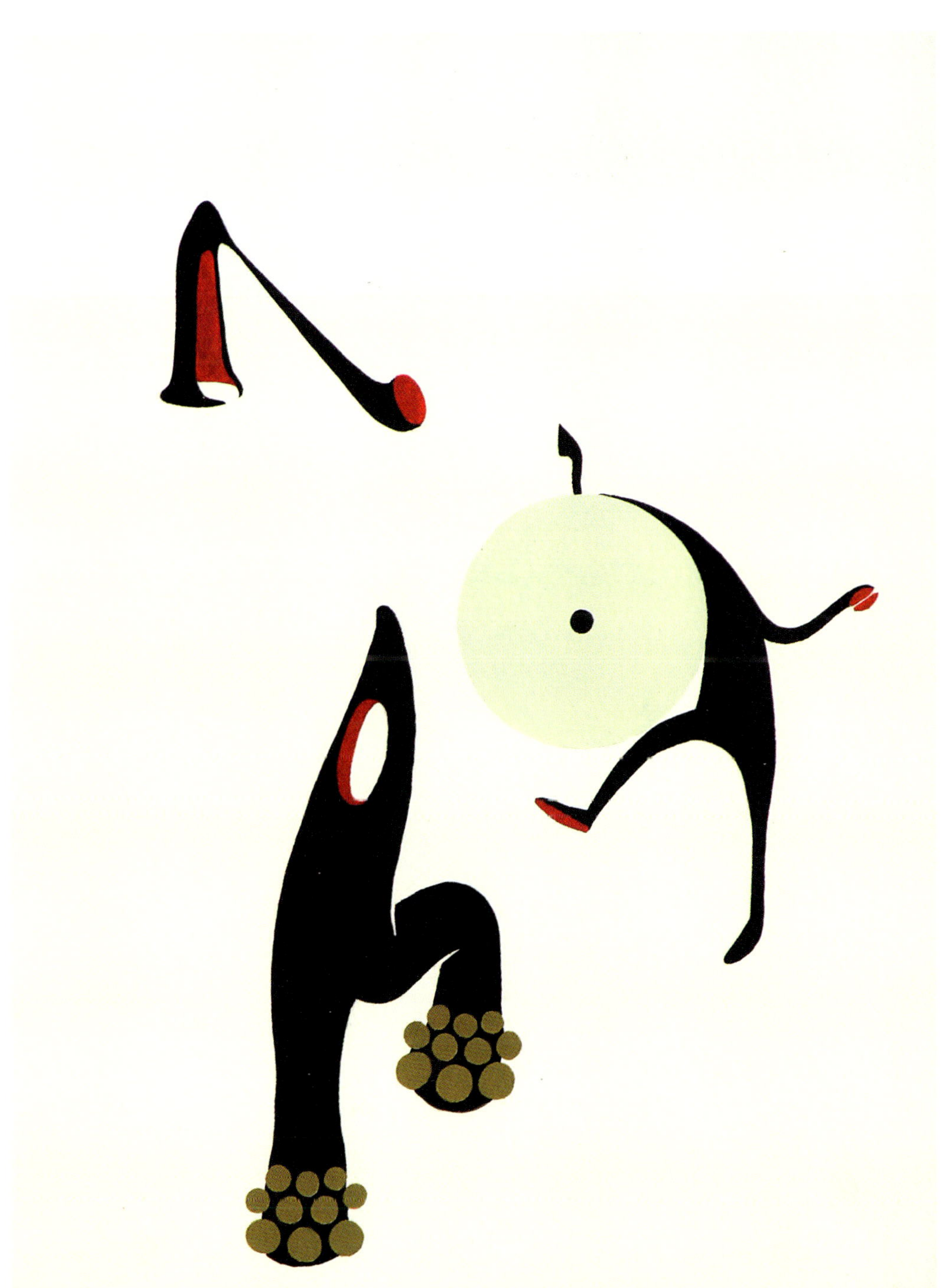

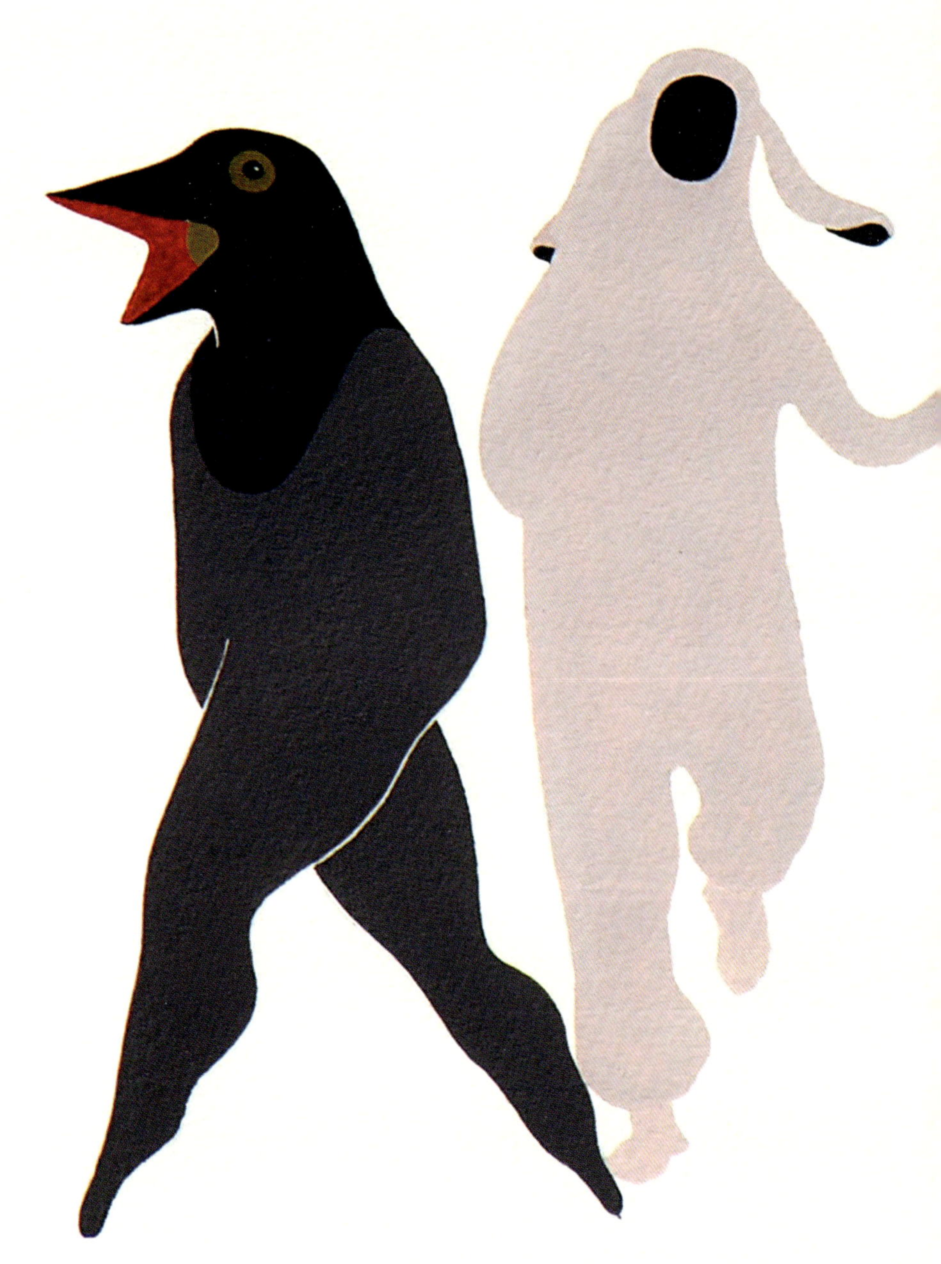

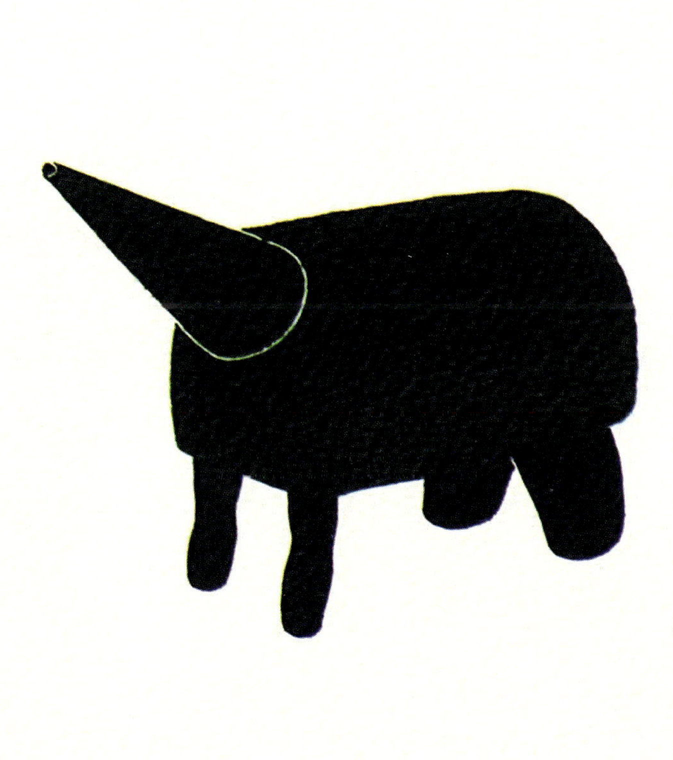

Pages 32–33
Troupe
Acrylics on paper
30 x 40 cm
2007

Right
Hippo
Acrylics on paper
40 x 30 cm
2007

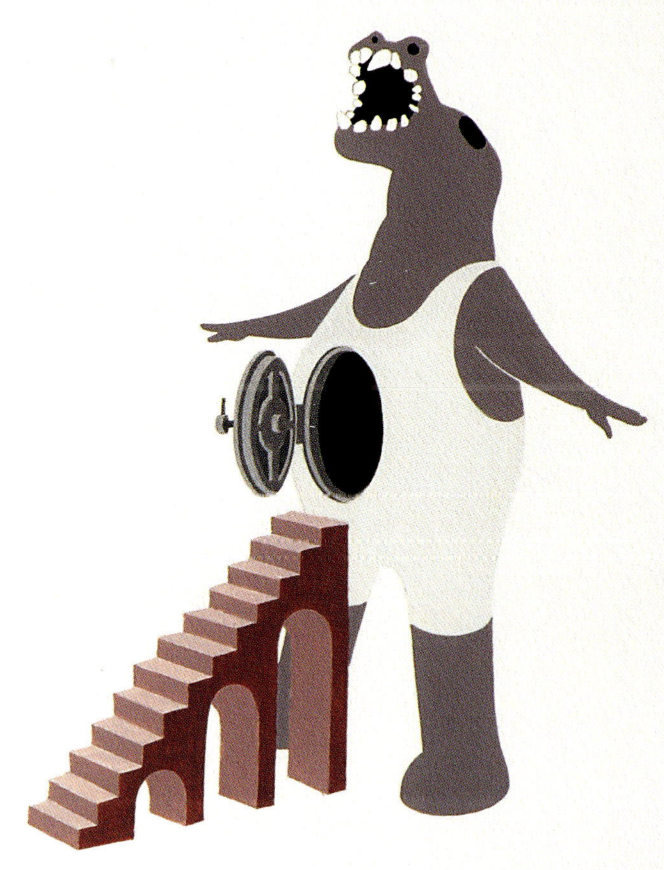

Right
Mother
Acrylics on paper
76 x 50 cm
2007

Bottom
Drawing for Mother
Ballpoint pen and
marker on paper
76.5 x 50.5 cm
2007

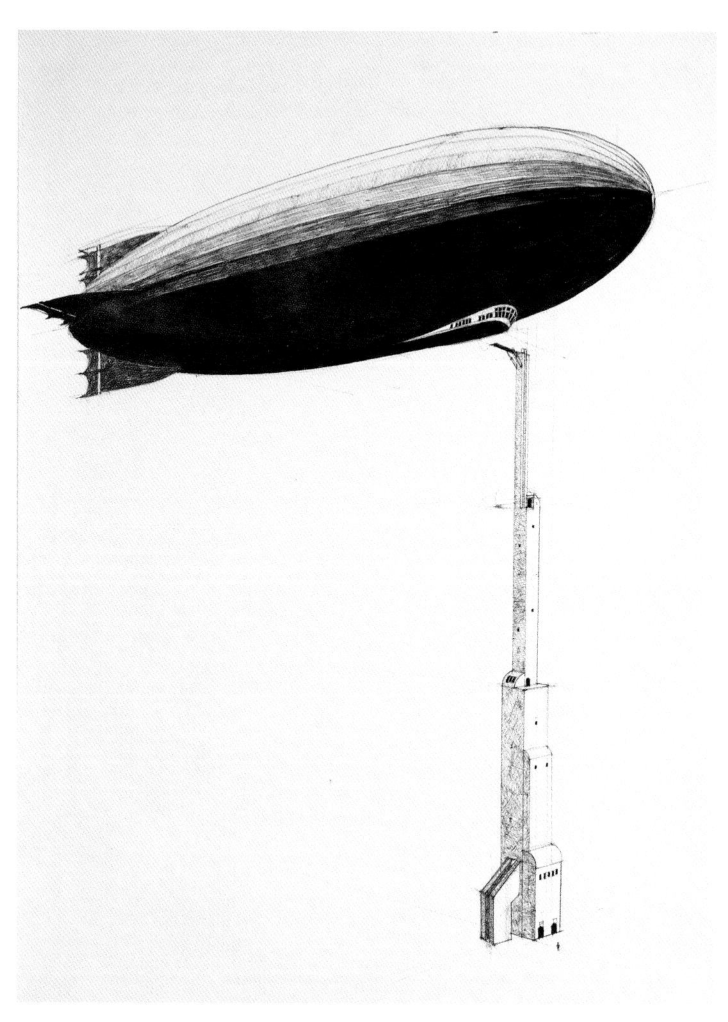

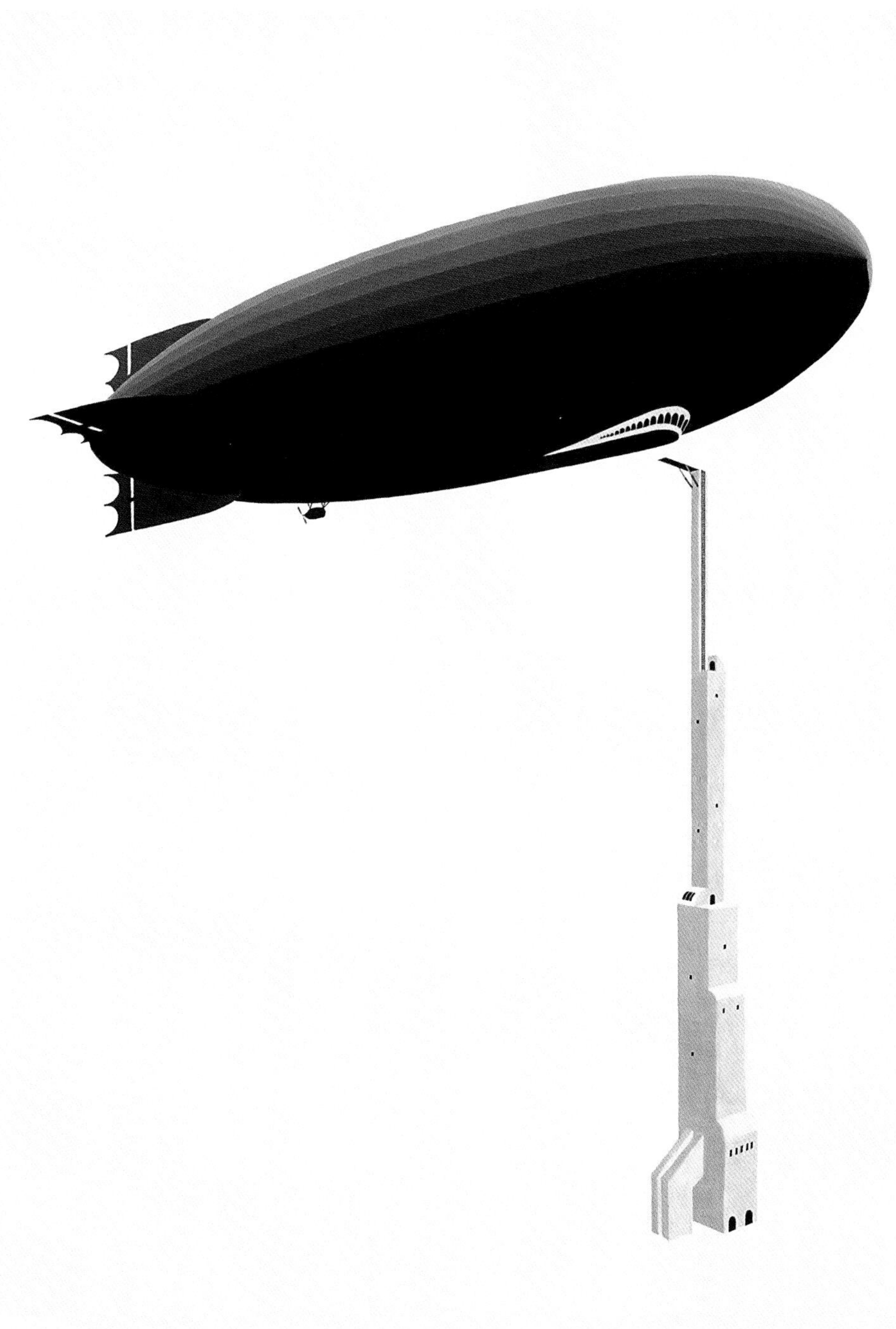

Altars
Acrylics on paper
40 x 30 cm
2007

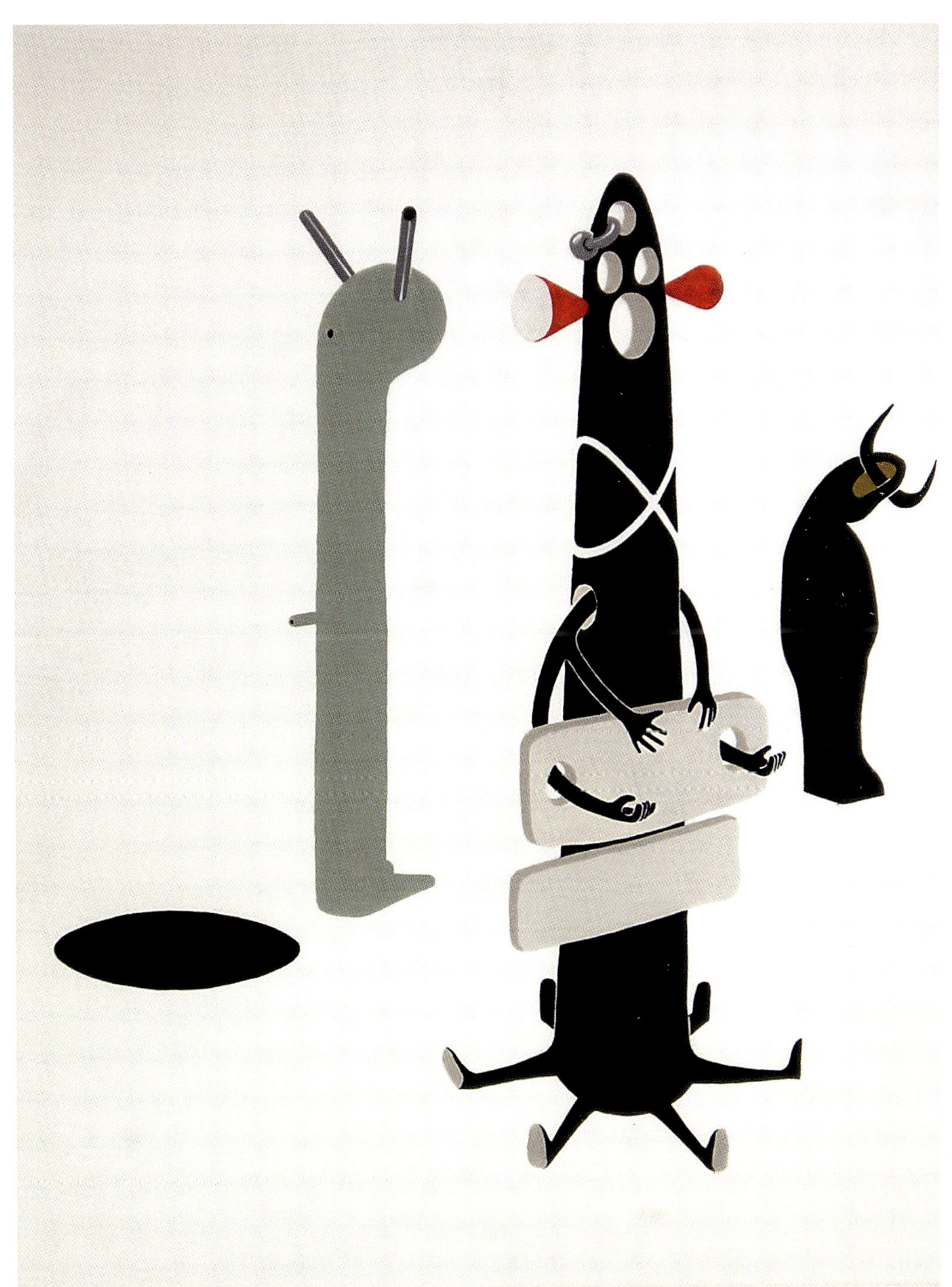

Reverie
Acrylics on paper
30 x 40 cm
2007

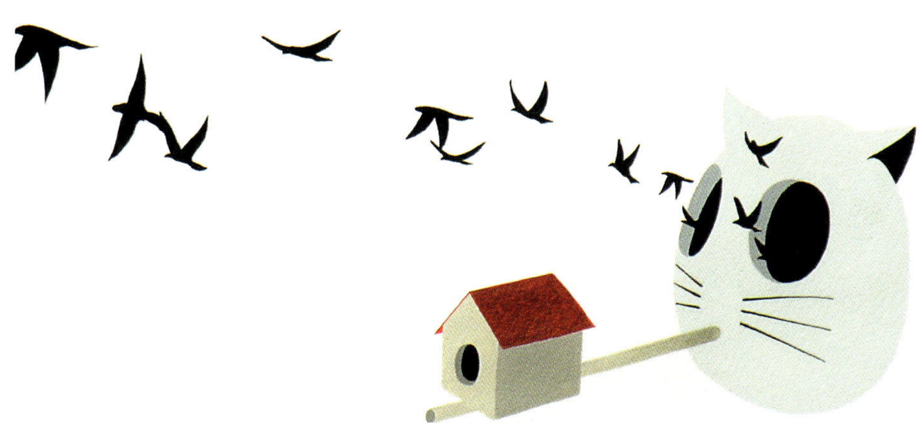

Derelict
Acrylics on paper
76 x 50 cm
2007

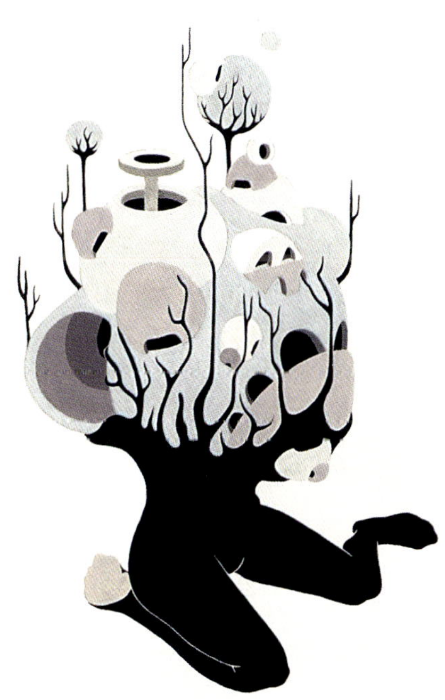

Standoff
Acrylics on paper
59 x 44 cm
2007

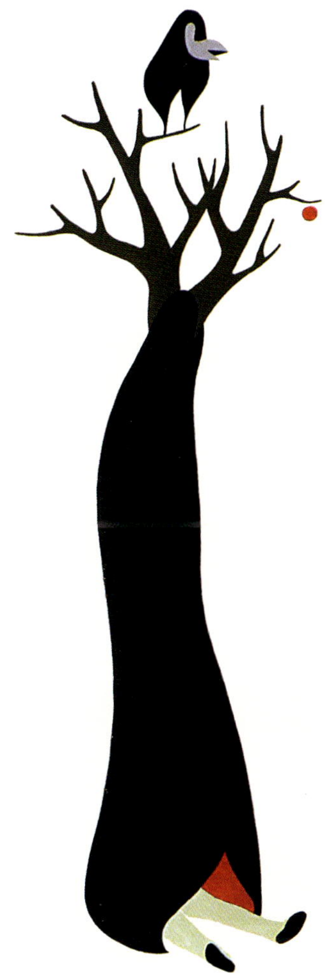
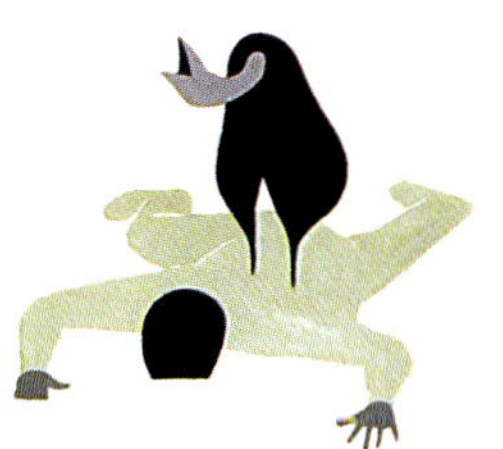

Purgatory
Acrylics on paper
76 x 50 cm
2007

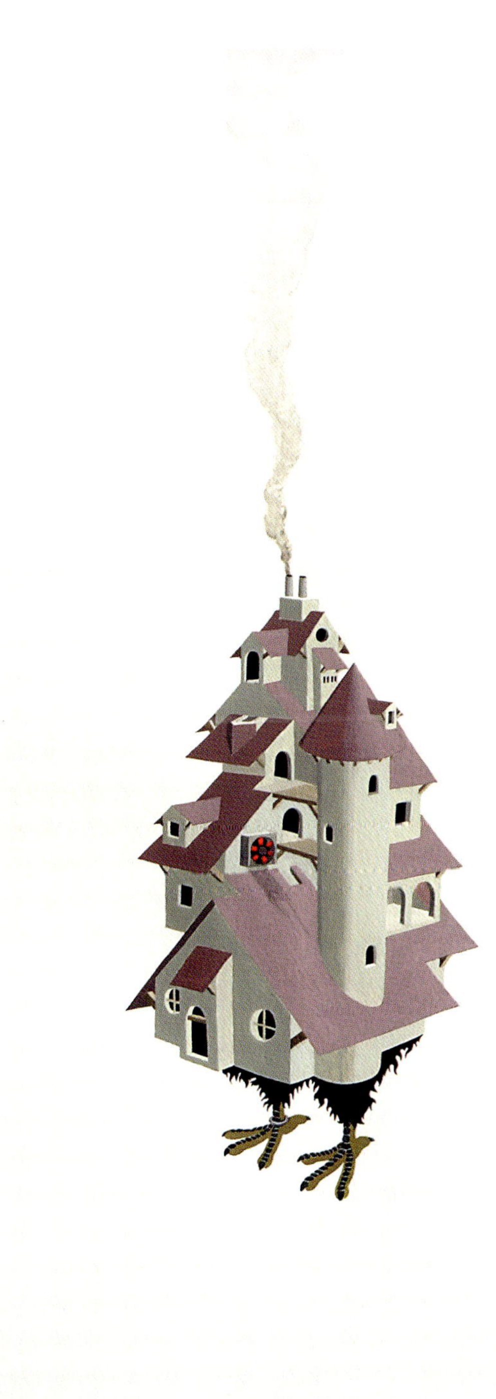

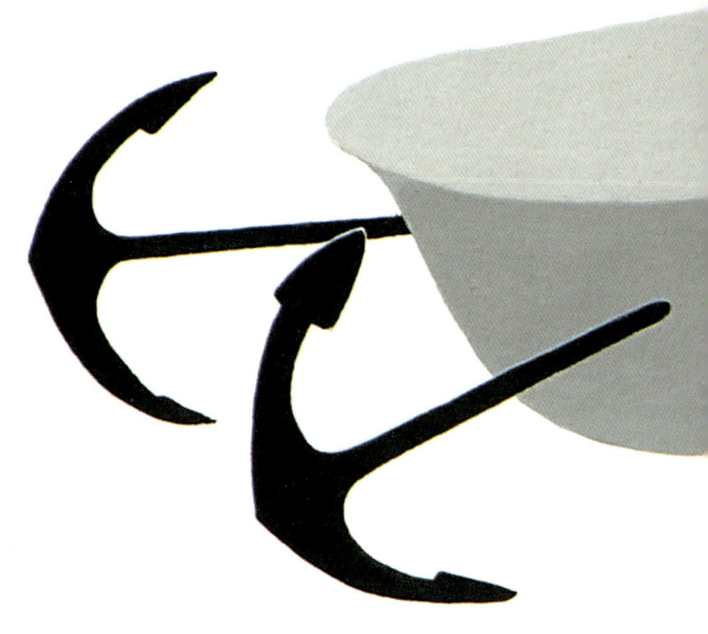

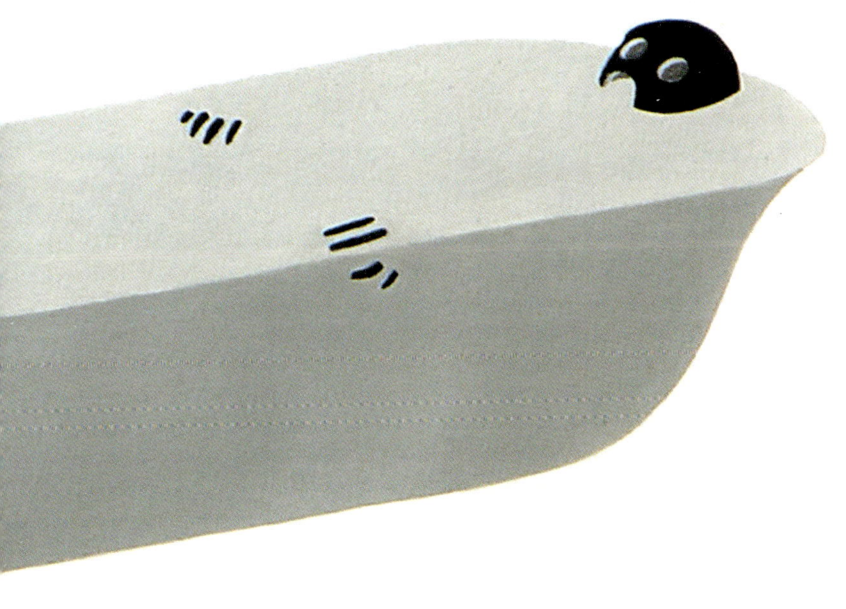

Pages 48–49
Boatman
Acrylics on paper
30 x 40 cm
2007

Right
Siren
Acrylics on paper
40 x 30 cm
2007

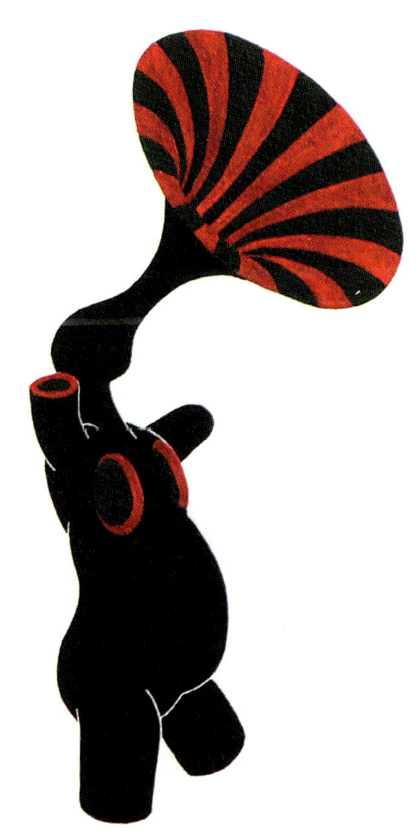

Fixed
Acrylics on paper
40 x 30 cm
2007

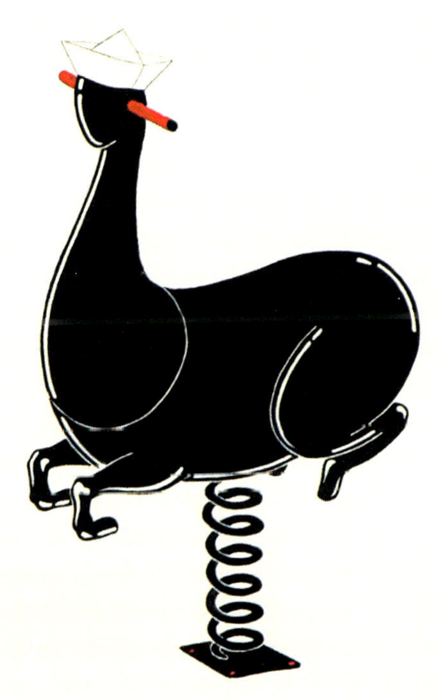

Totem
Acrylics on paper
40 x 30 cm
2007

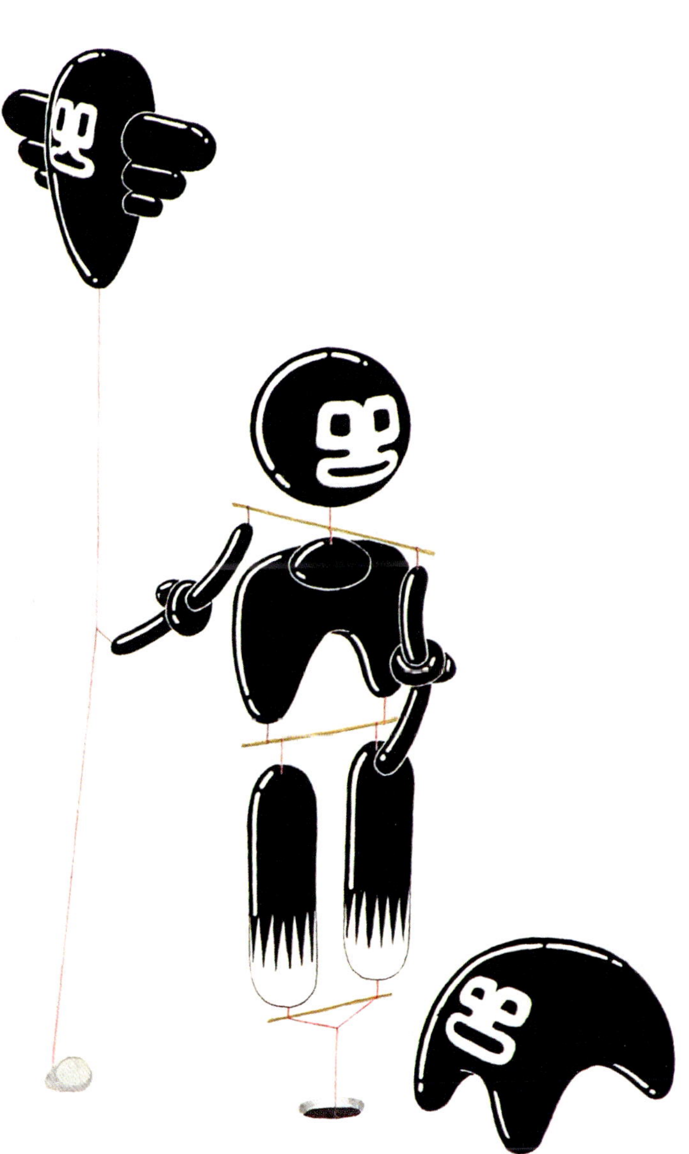

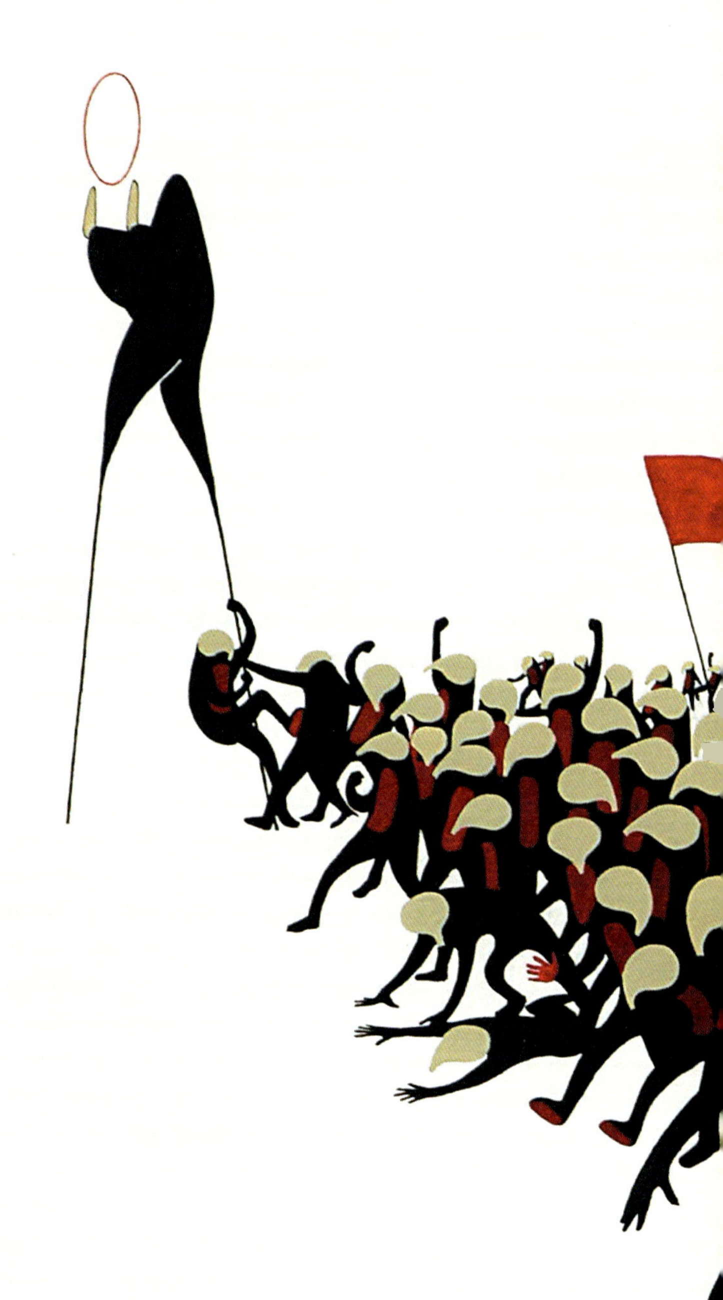

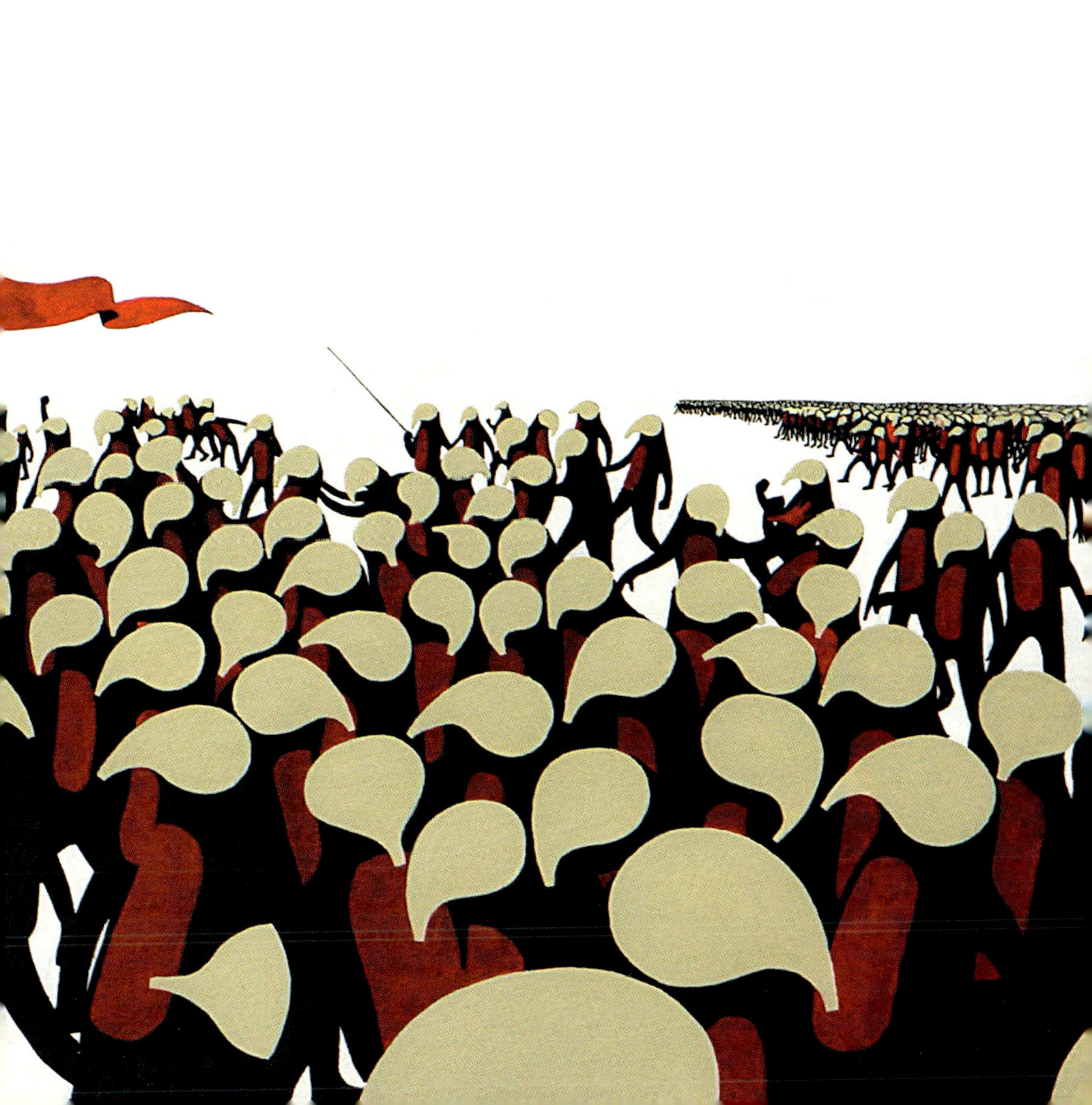

Pages 56–57
Piper
Acrylics on paper
50 x 76 cm
2007

Right
Ritual
Acrylics on paper
40 x 30 cm
2007

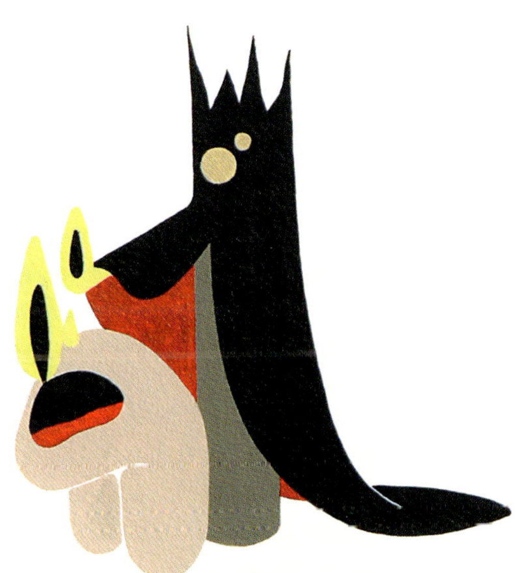
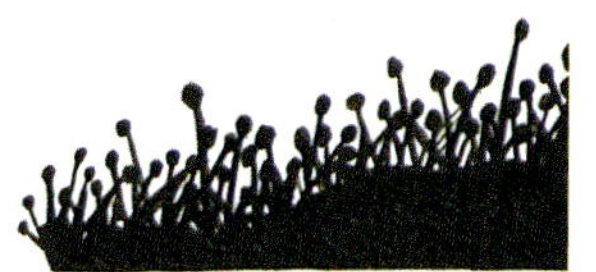
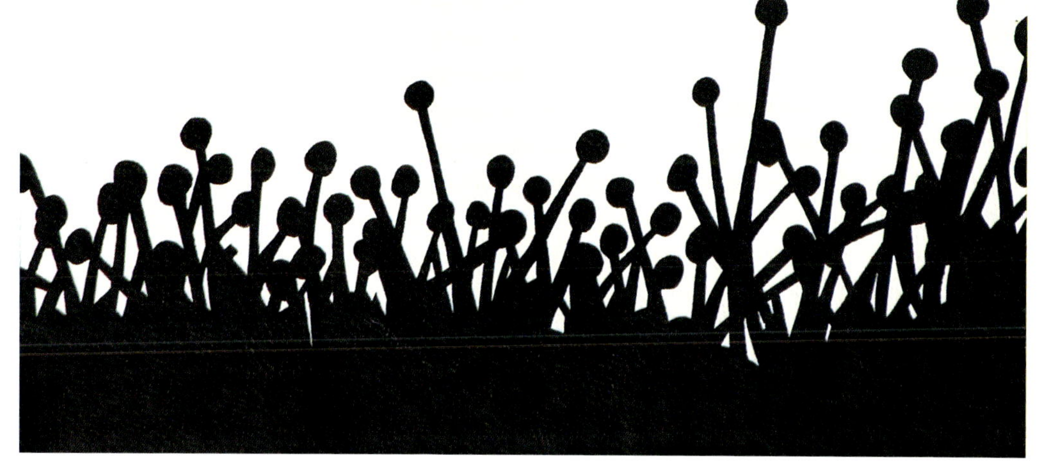

Echo
Acrylics on paper
40 x 30 cm
2007

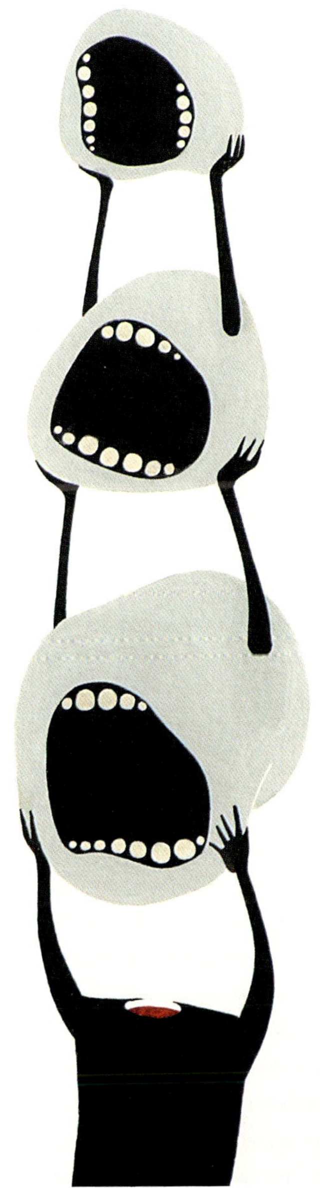

Sentinel
Acrylics on paper
40 x 30 cm
2007

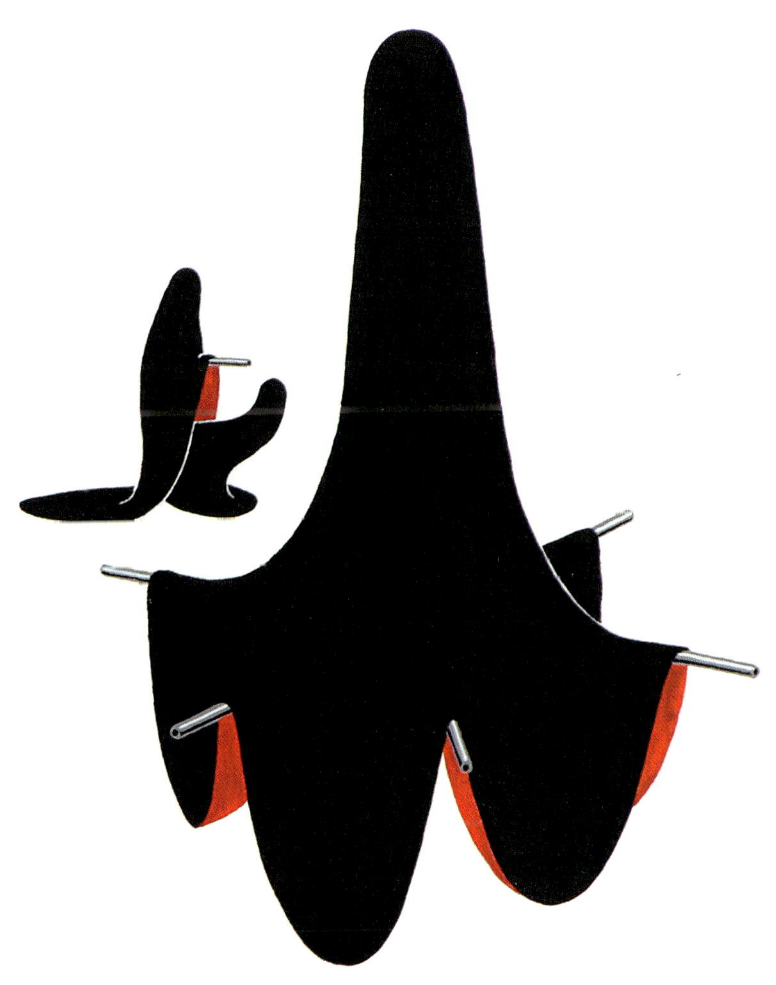

Untitled (delirious)
Acrylics on paper
40 x 30 cm
2007

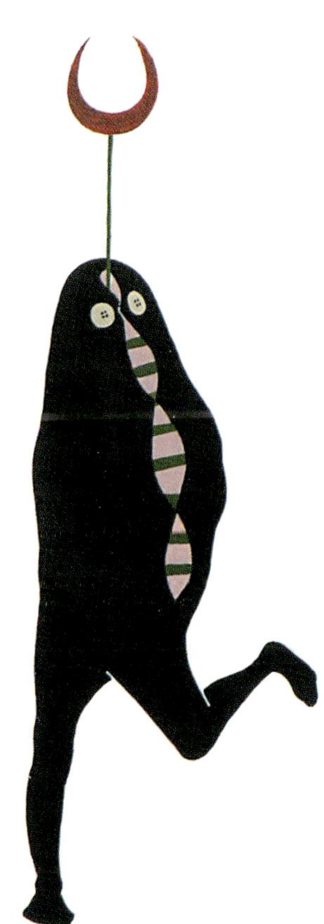

Weather man
Acrylics on paper
40 x 30 cm
2007

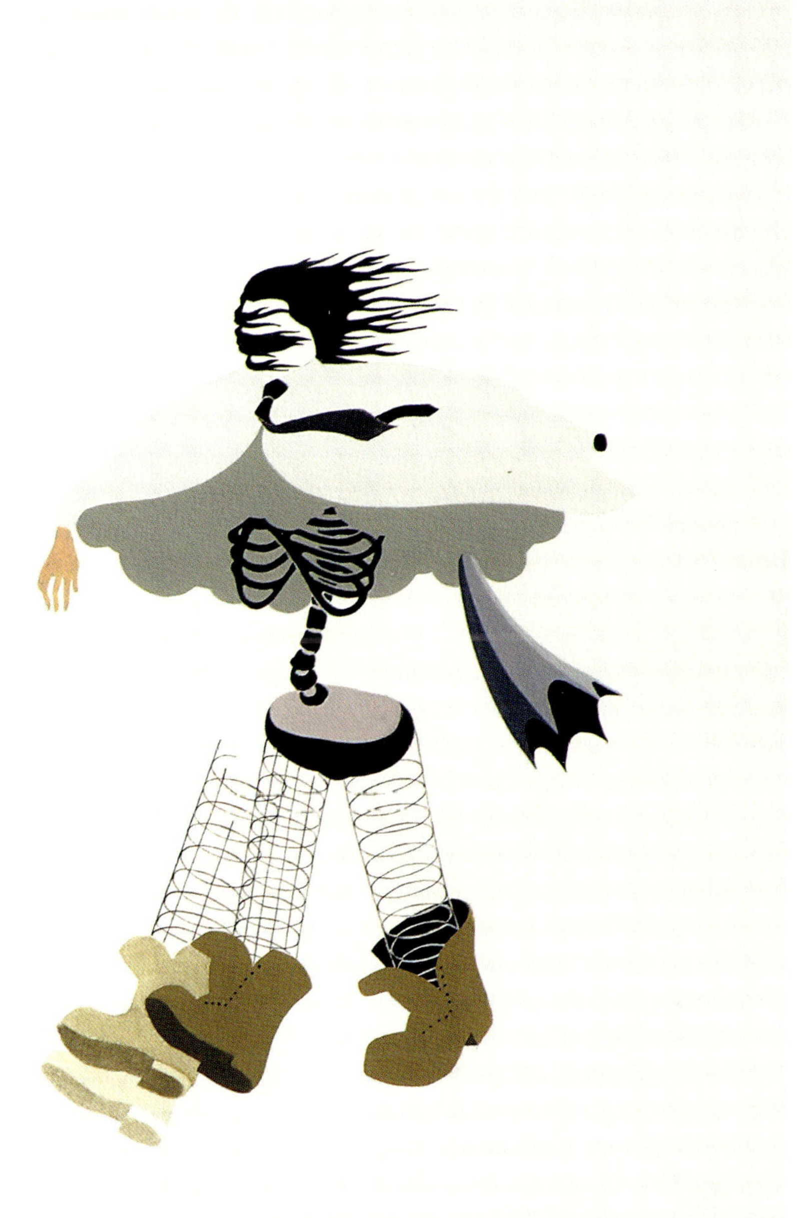

Fatman
Acrylics on paper
40 x 30 cm
2007

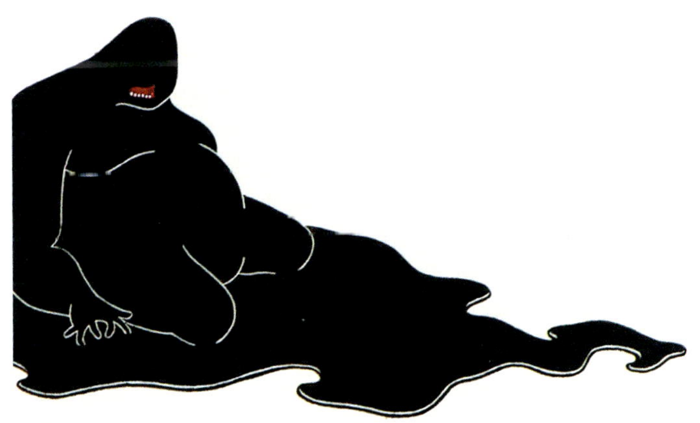

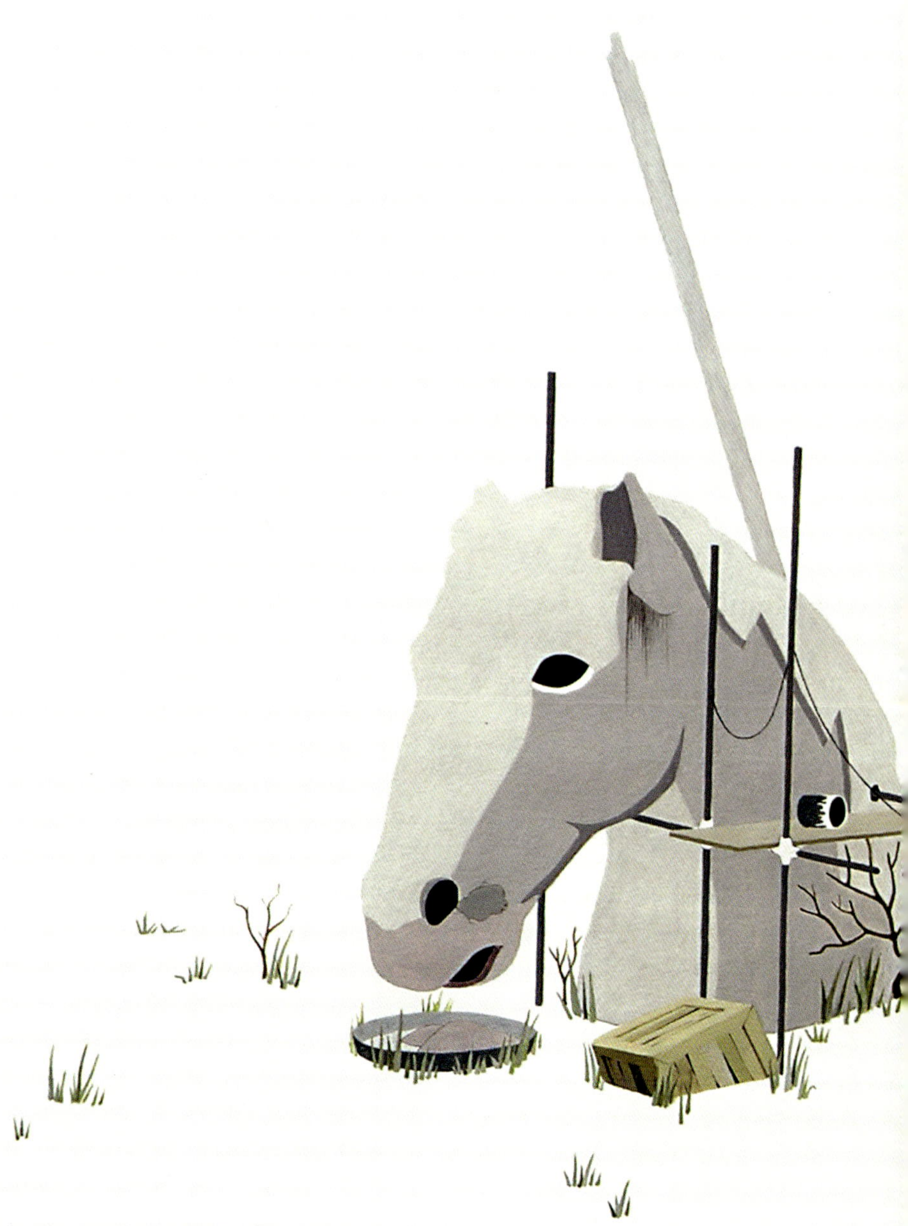

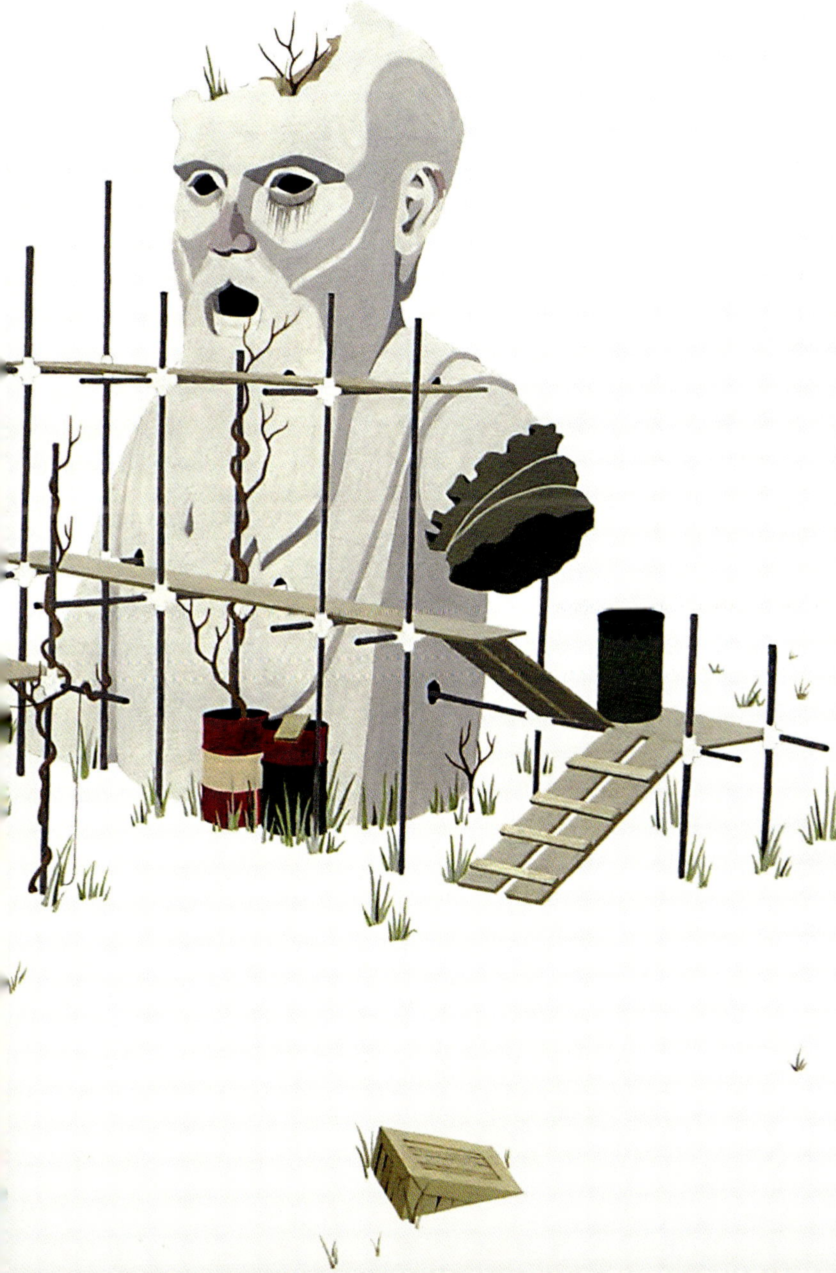

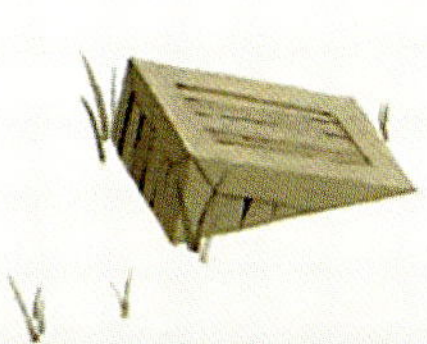

Pages 70–71
Site
Acrylics on paper
76 x 102 cm
2007

Bottom
Drawing for Site
Ballpoint pen
on paper
50.5 x 76.5 cm
2007

Right
Balloon Building
Ballpoint pen
on paper
106.6 x 78.74 cm
2007

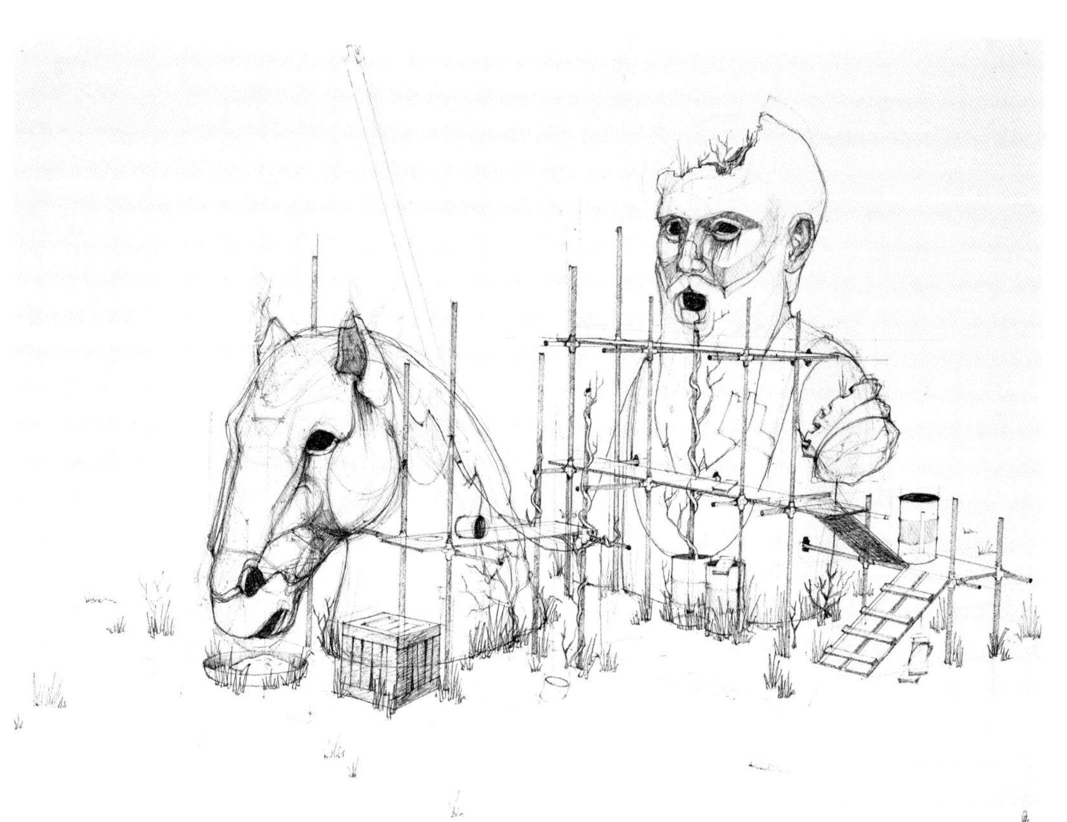

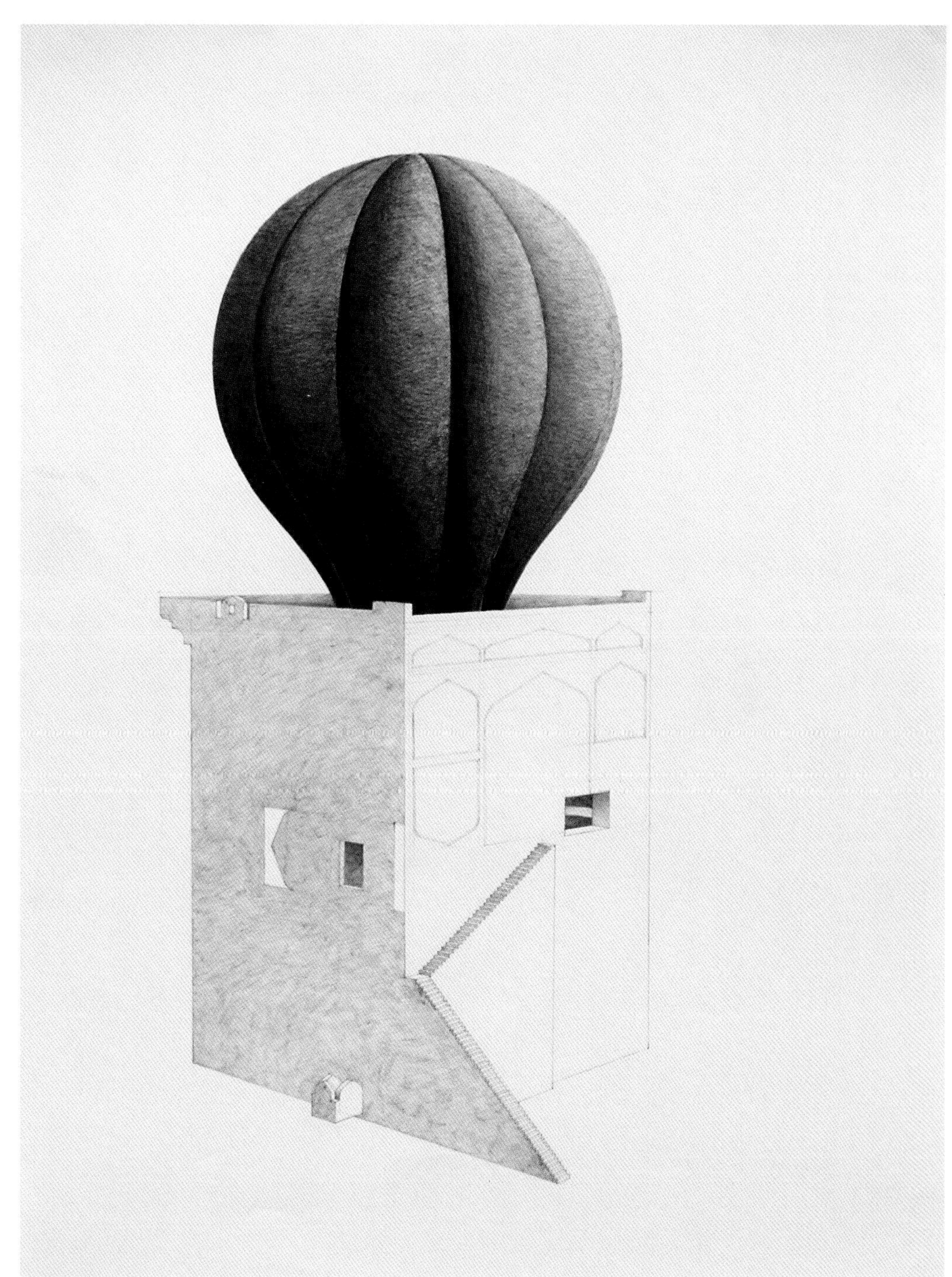

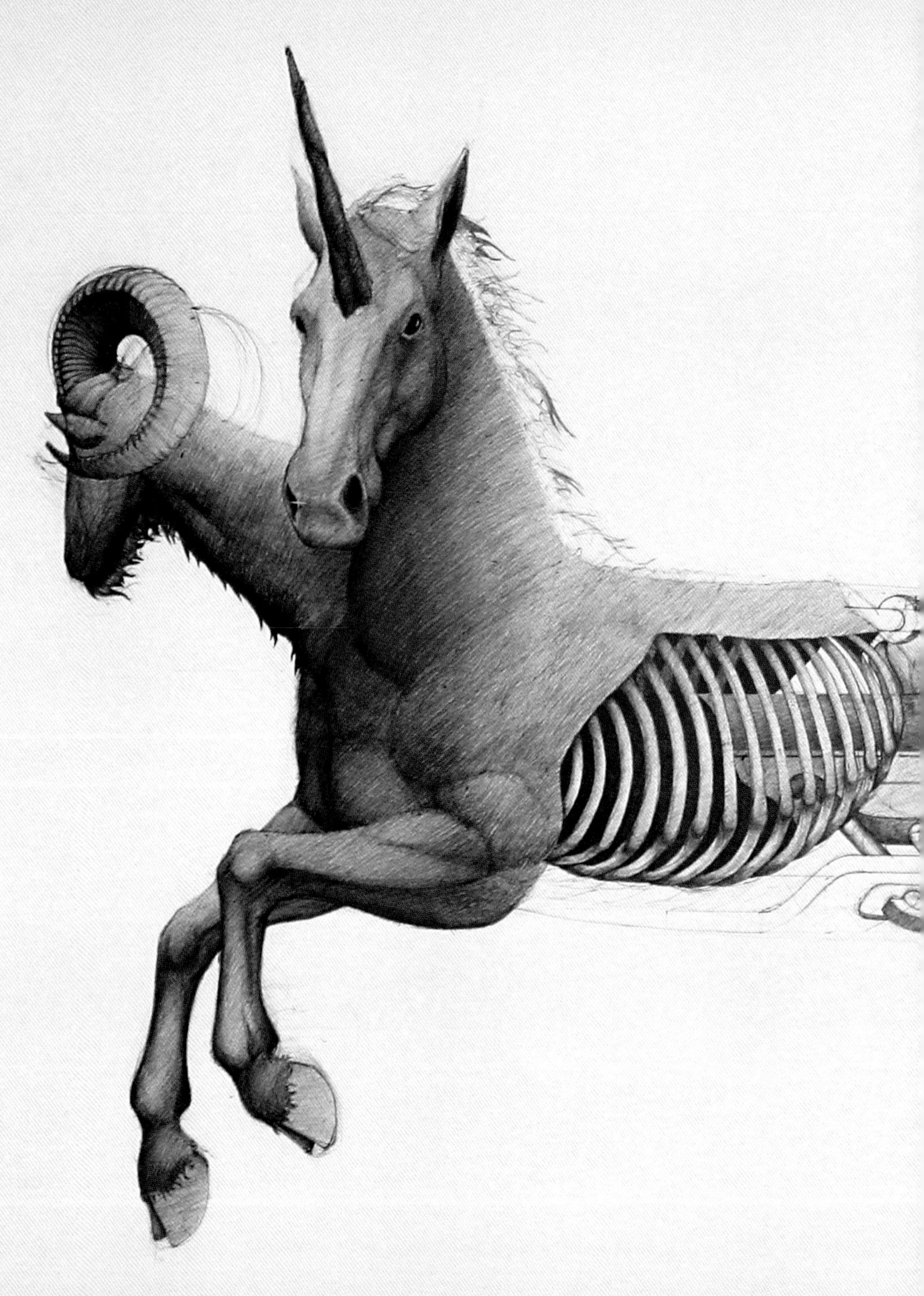

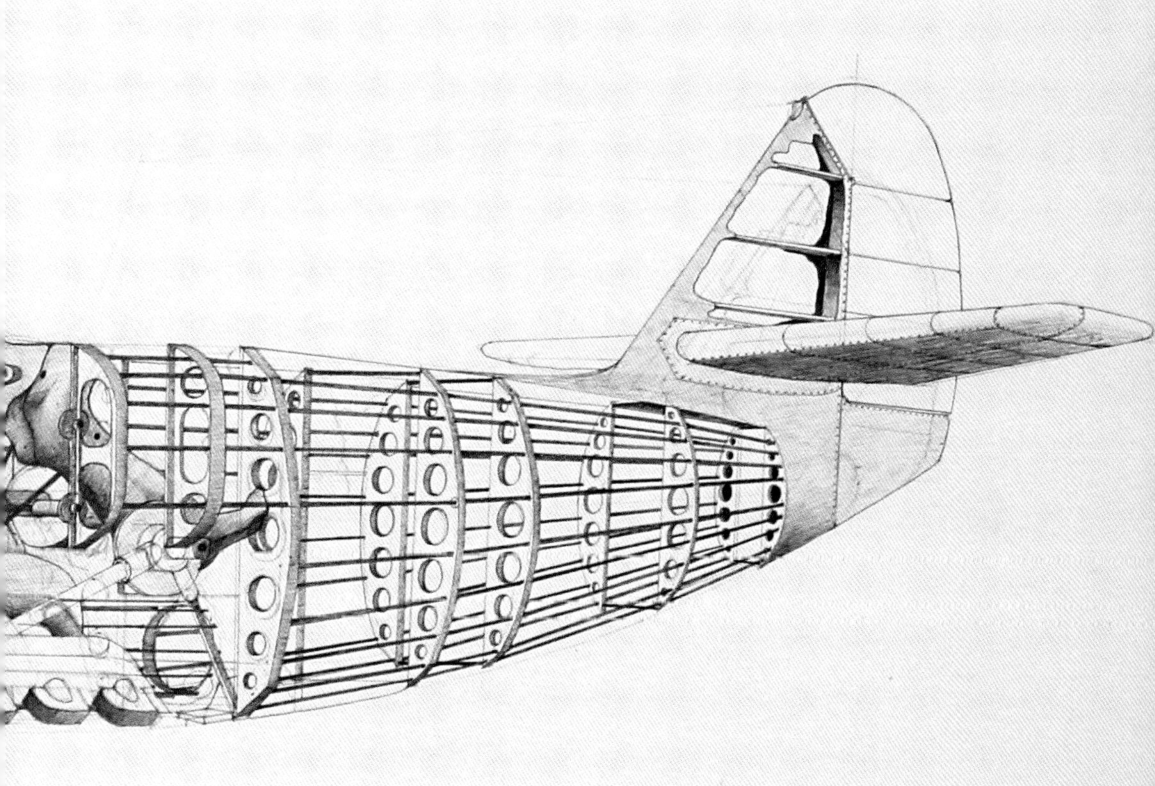

Pages 74–75
Untitled drawing
Ballpoint pen
on paper
78.7 x 106.8 cm
2007

Right
Echo
Acrylics on paper
76 x 101 cm
2008

Right
Parameter
Felt tip pen and
pencil on paper
213 x 152 cm
2008

Pages 80–81
Parameter (detail)
Felt tip pen and
pencil on paper
213 x 152 cm
2008

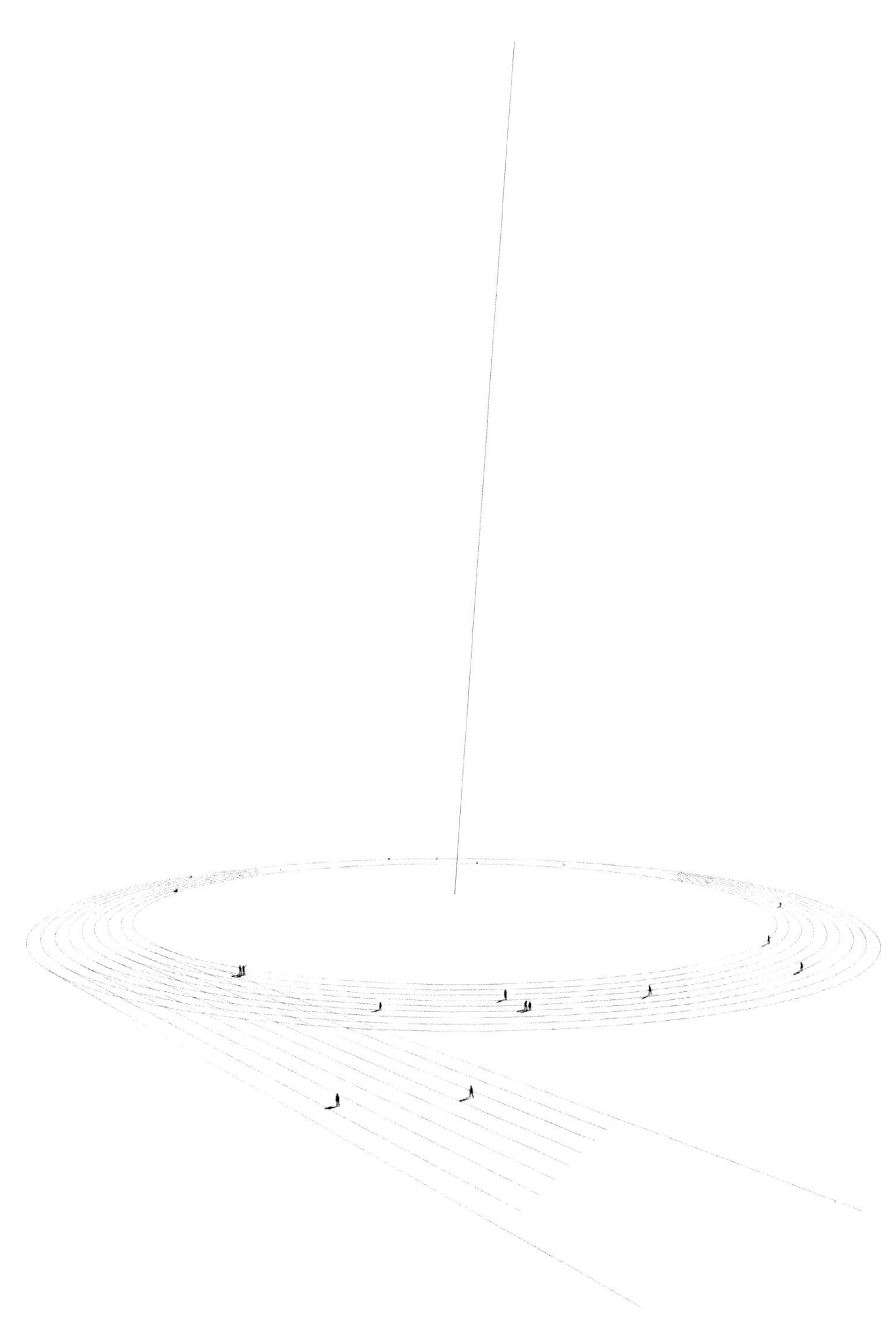

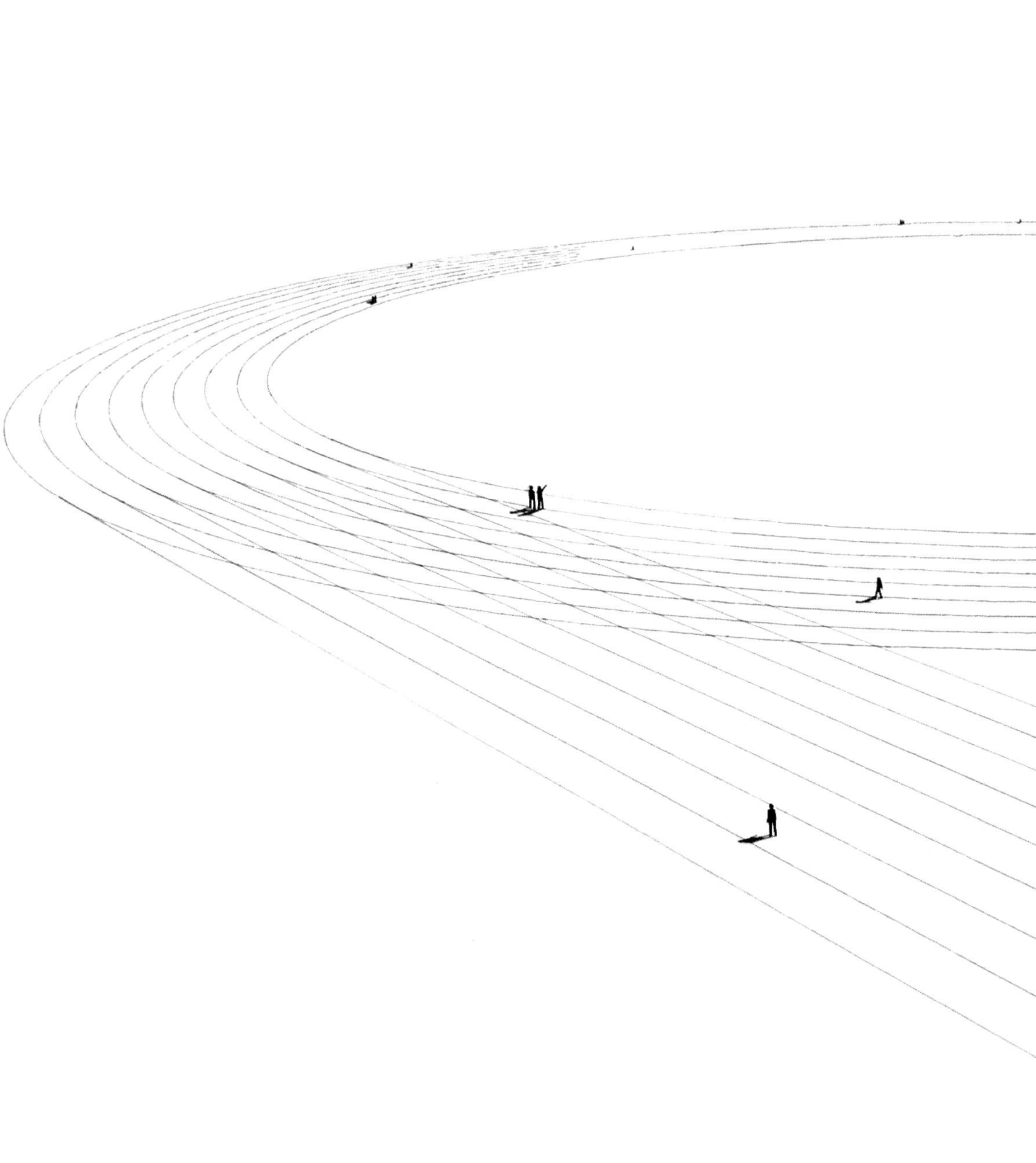

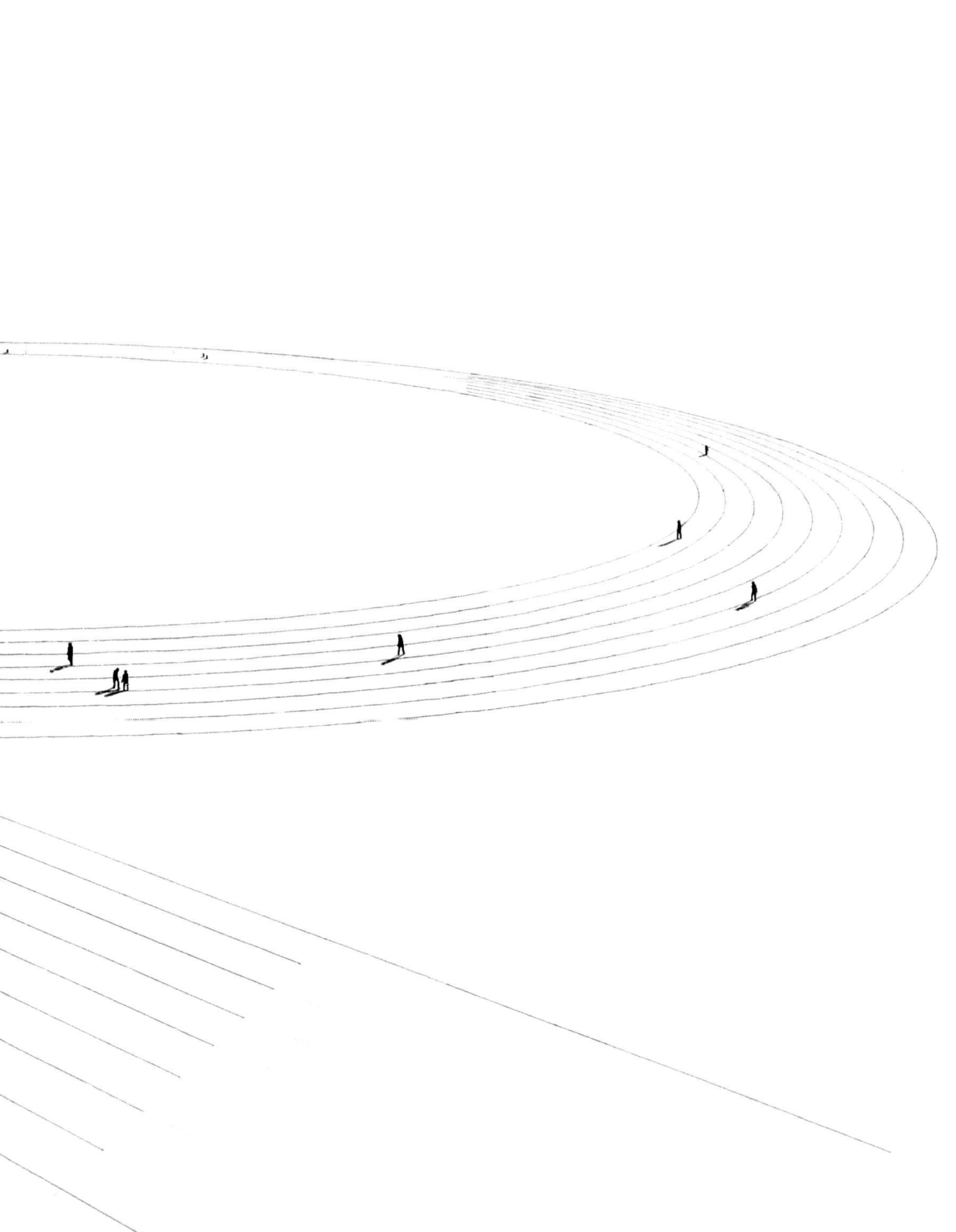

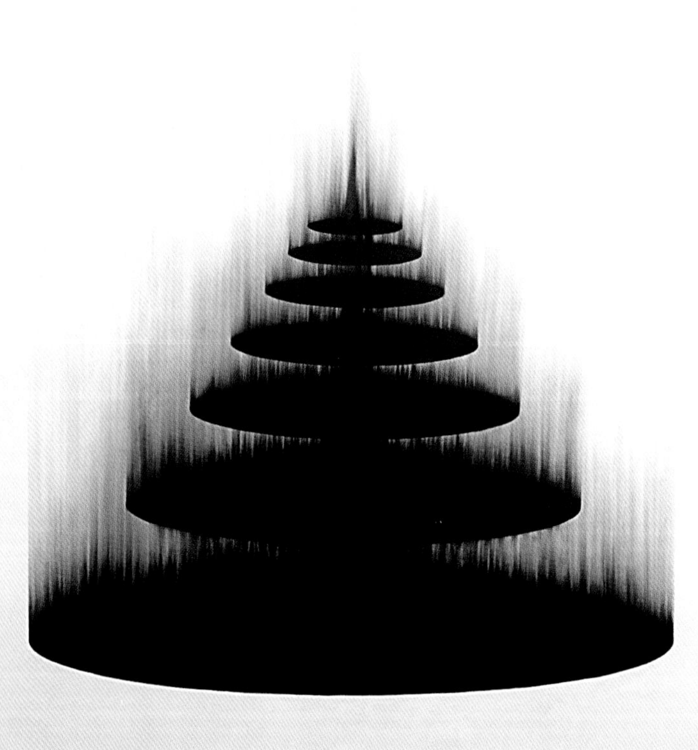

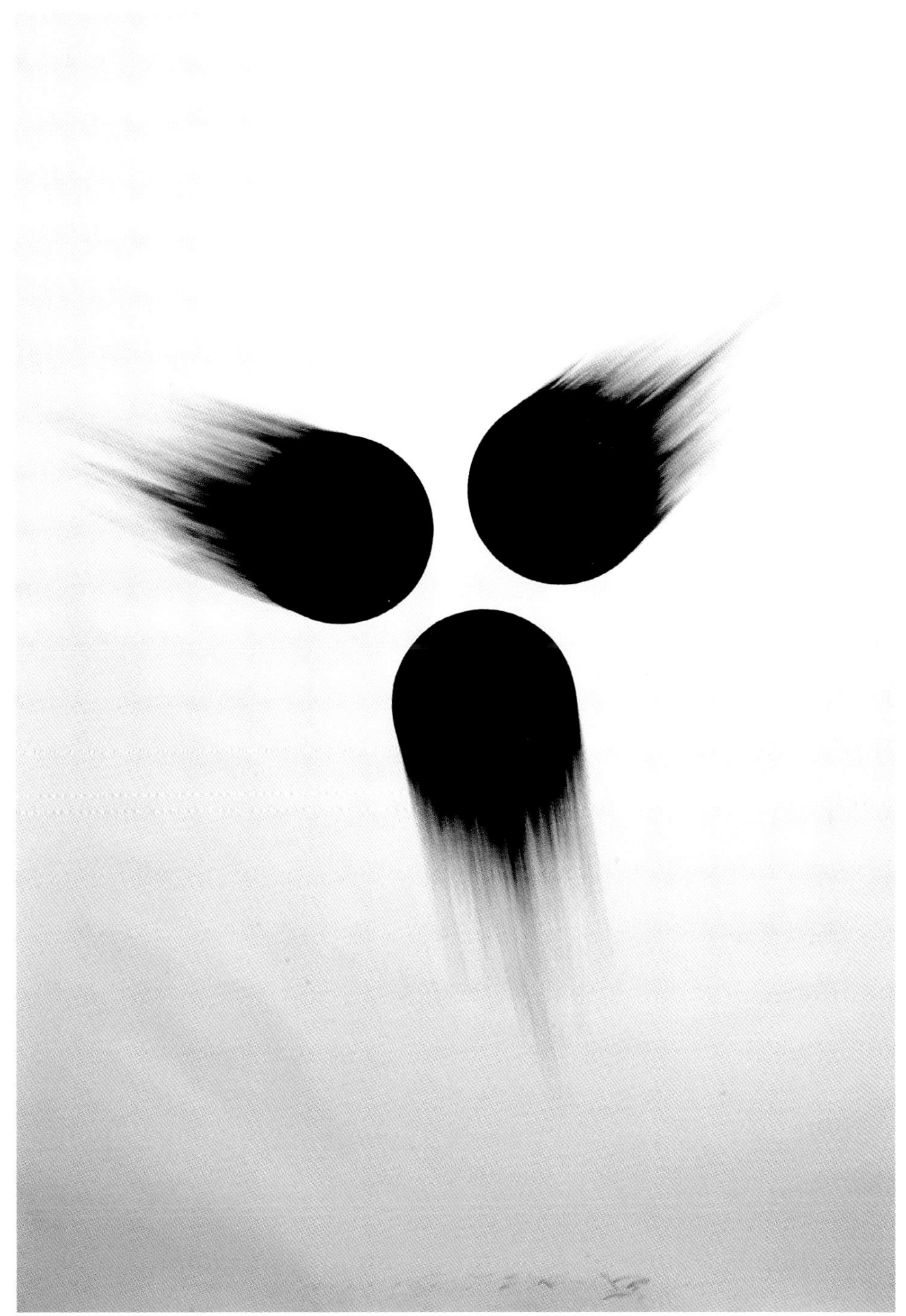

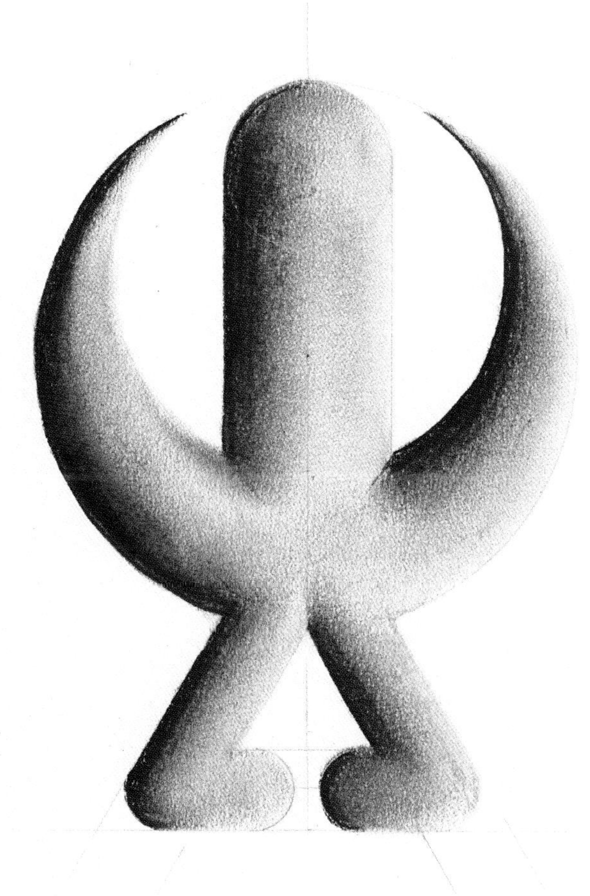

Malediction
Indian ink on paper
155 x 122 cm
2009

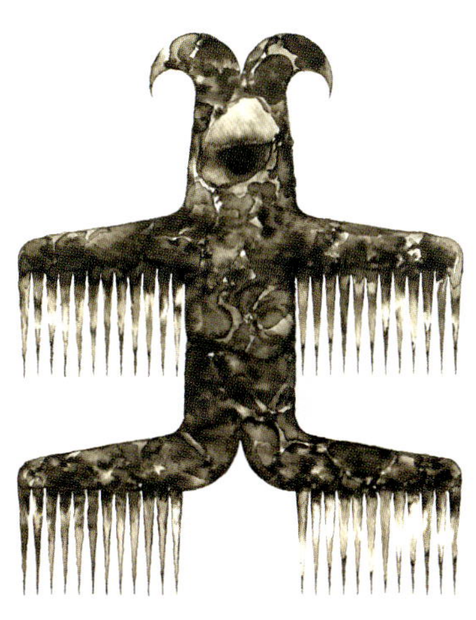

Untitled
Screen print on paper
91.44 x 66.80 cm
Edition of 5 + 1 AP
2009

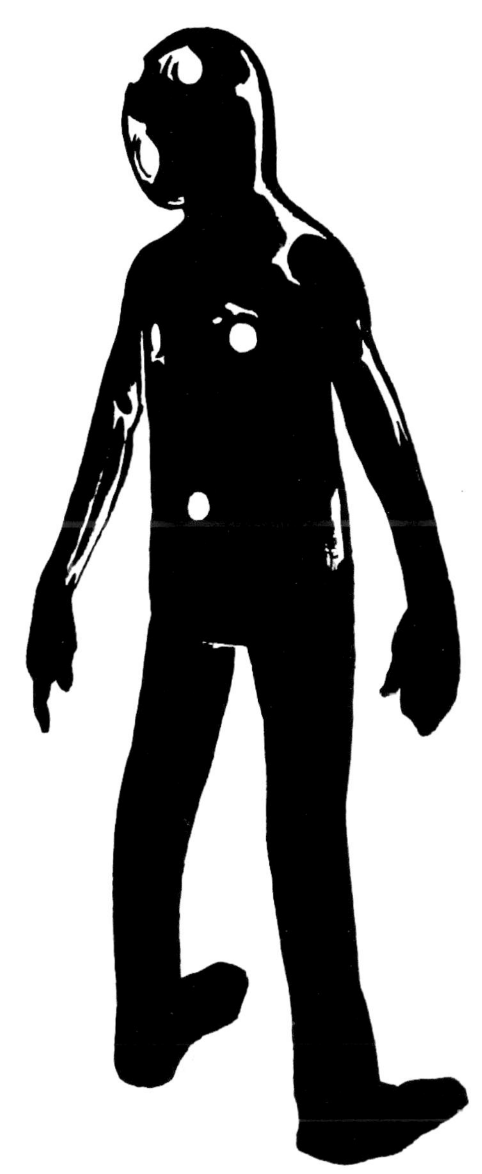

Sleeper
Acrylics on paper
41.91 x 58.42 cm
2008

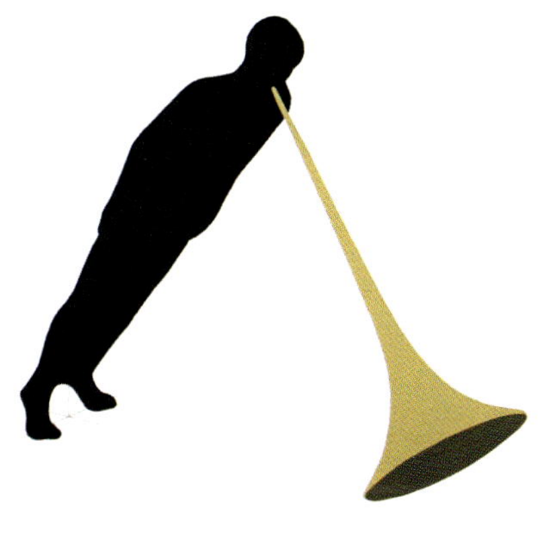

Wizard
Acrylics on paper
76 x 56 cm
2007

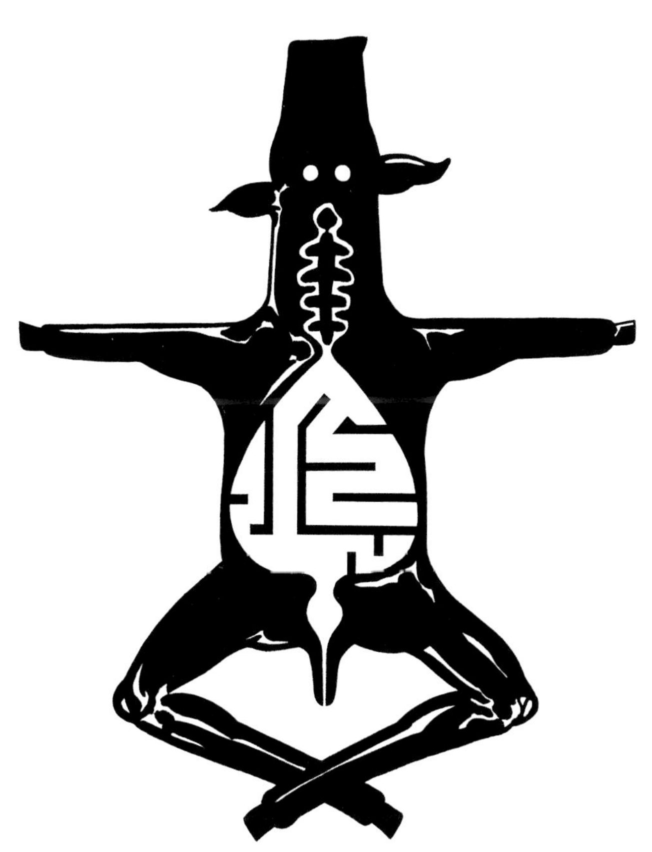

Frogboy
Acrylics on paper
76 x 56 cm
2007

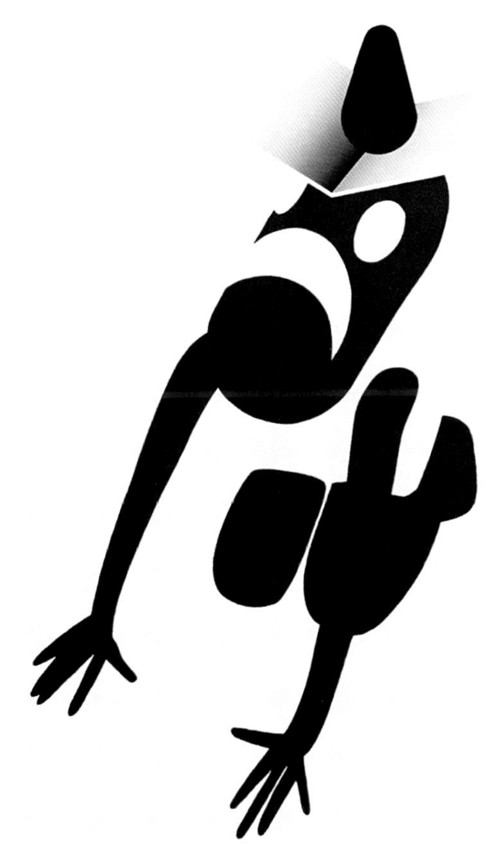

Vest
Acrylics on paper
76 x 56 cm
2007

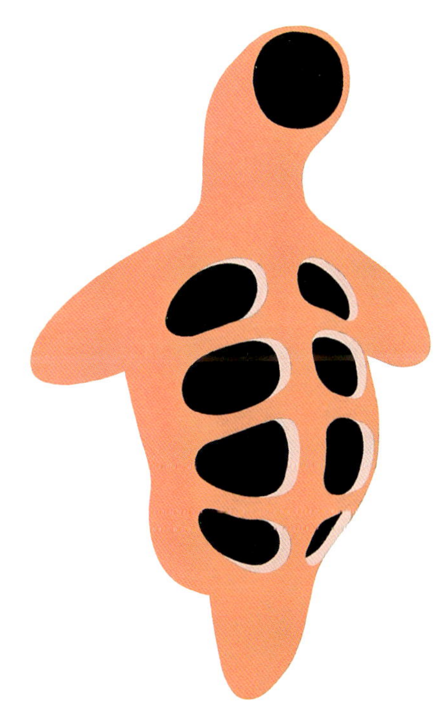

Fair Trade
Acrylics on paper
76 x 56 cm
2007

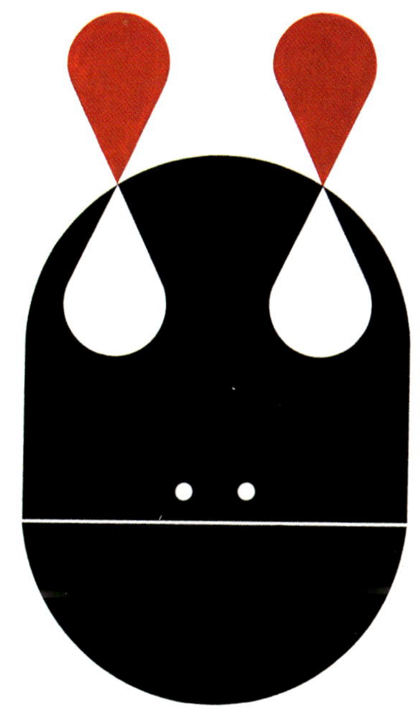

Untitled
Acrylics on canvas
76 x 56 cm
2007

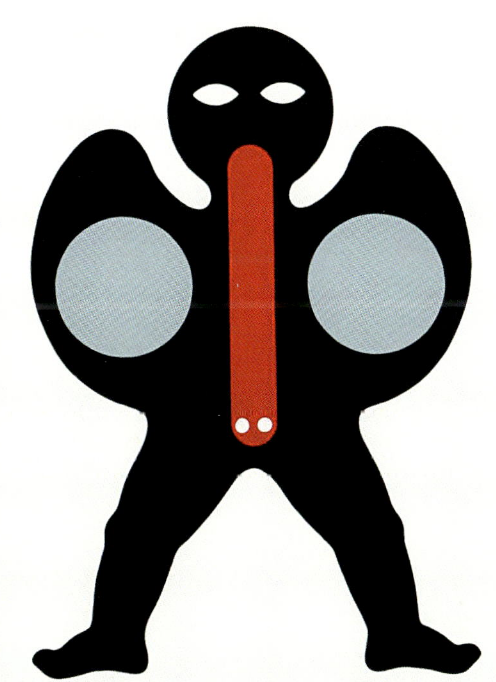

Right
Vessel
Acrylics on paper
76 x 56 cm
2007

Bottom
Drawing for Vessel
Acrylics on paper
76 x 56 cm
2007

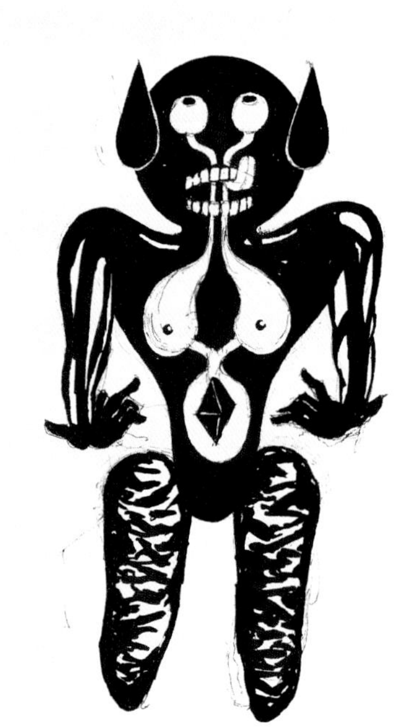

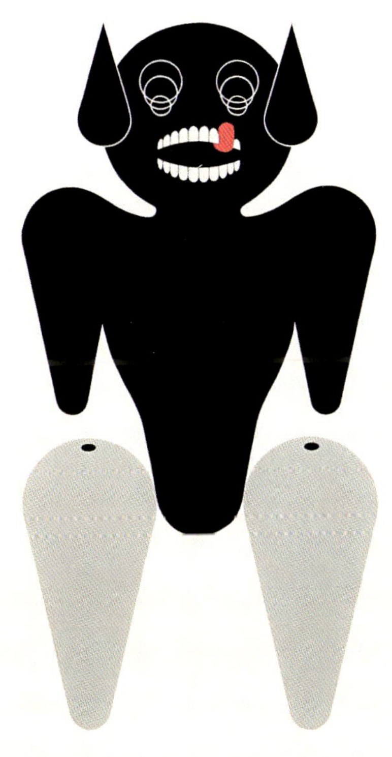

Untitled
Acrylics on paper
80 x 67 cm
2009

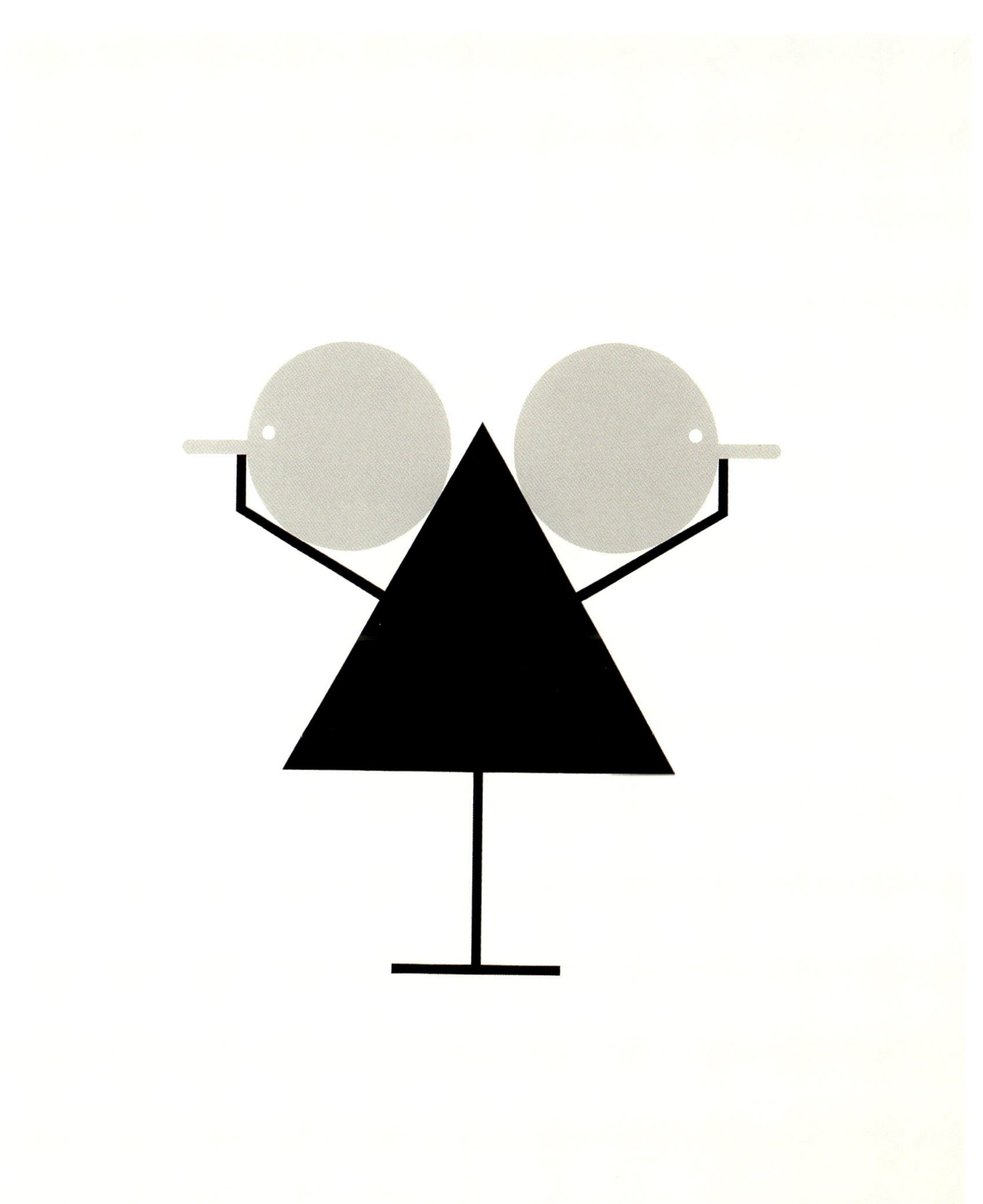

Augur
Acrylics on paper
102 x 67 cm
2009

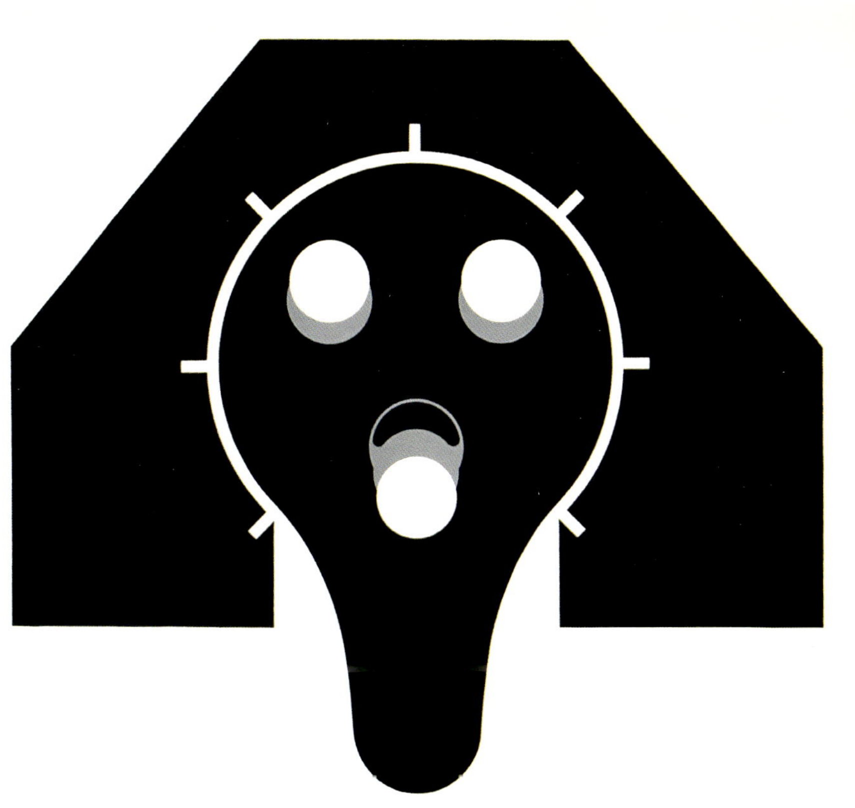

Watcher
Acrylics on paper
102 x 67 cm
2010

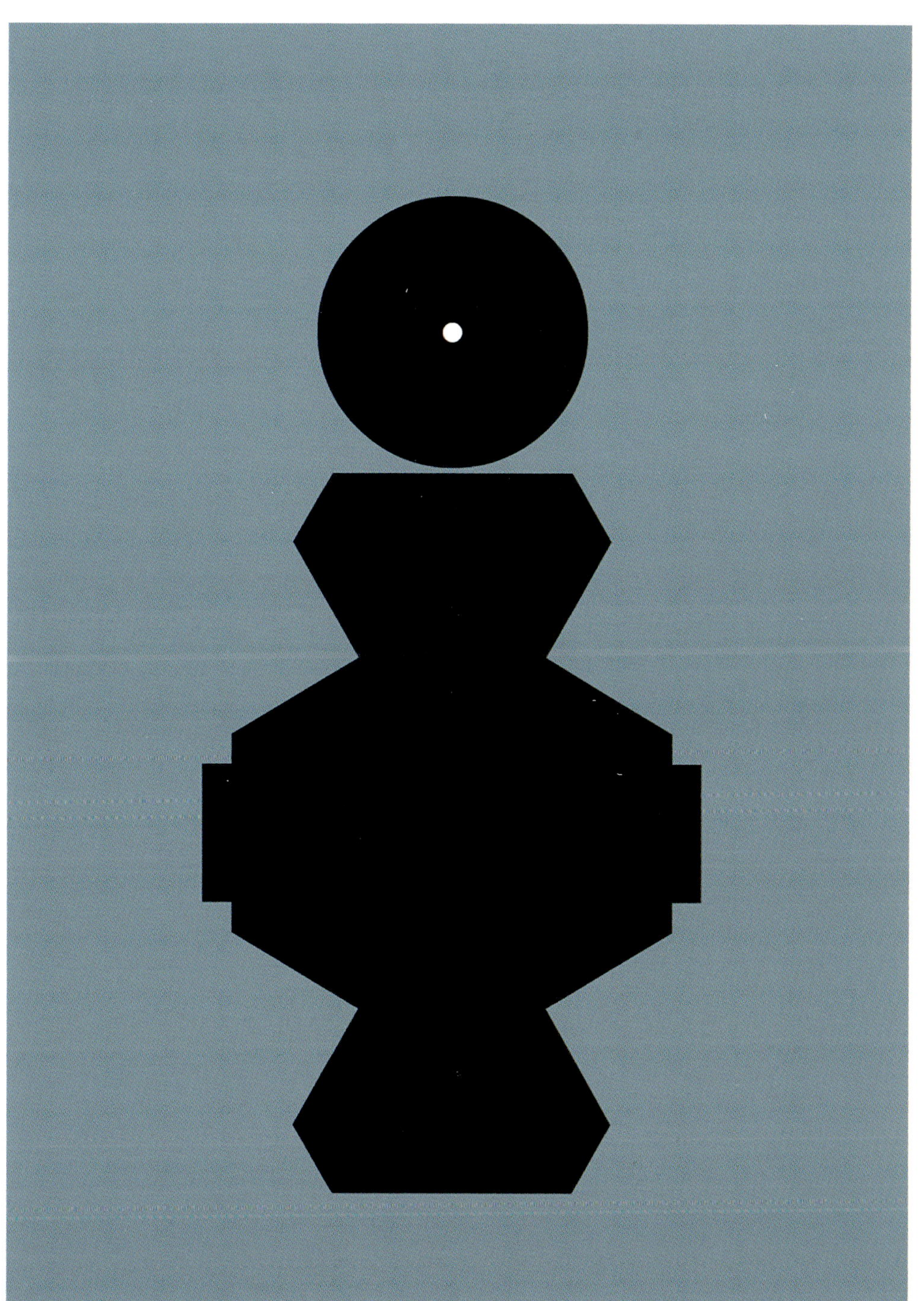

Plenitude
Acrylics on paper
122 x 152 cm
2009

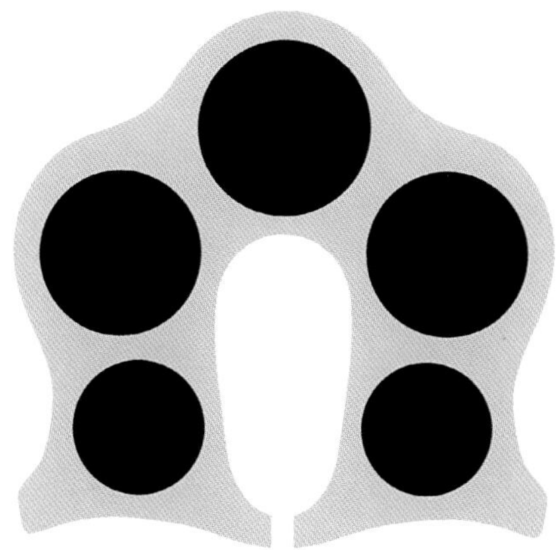

Lullaby
Acrylics on paper
152 x 122 cm
2009

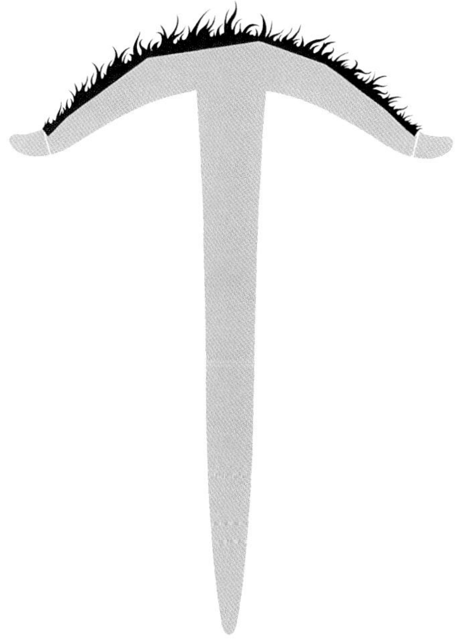

Reserve
Collage on paper
152 x 122 cm
2009

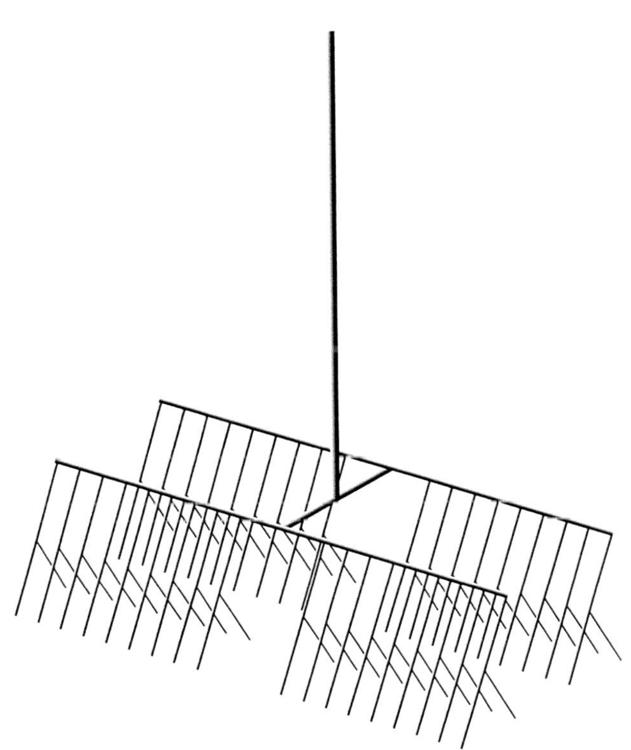

Bound
MDF and acrylics
42 x 30 x 6 cm
2009

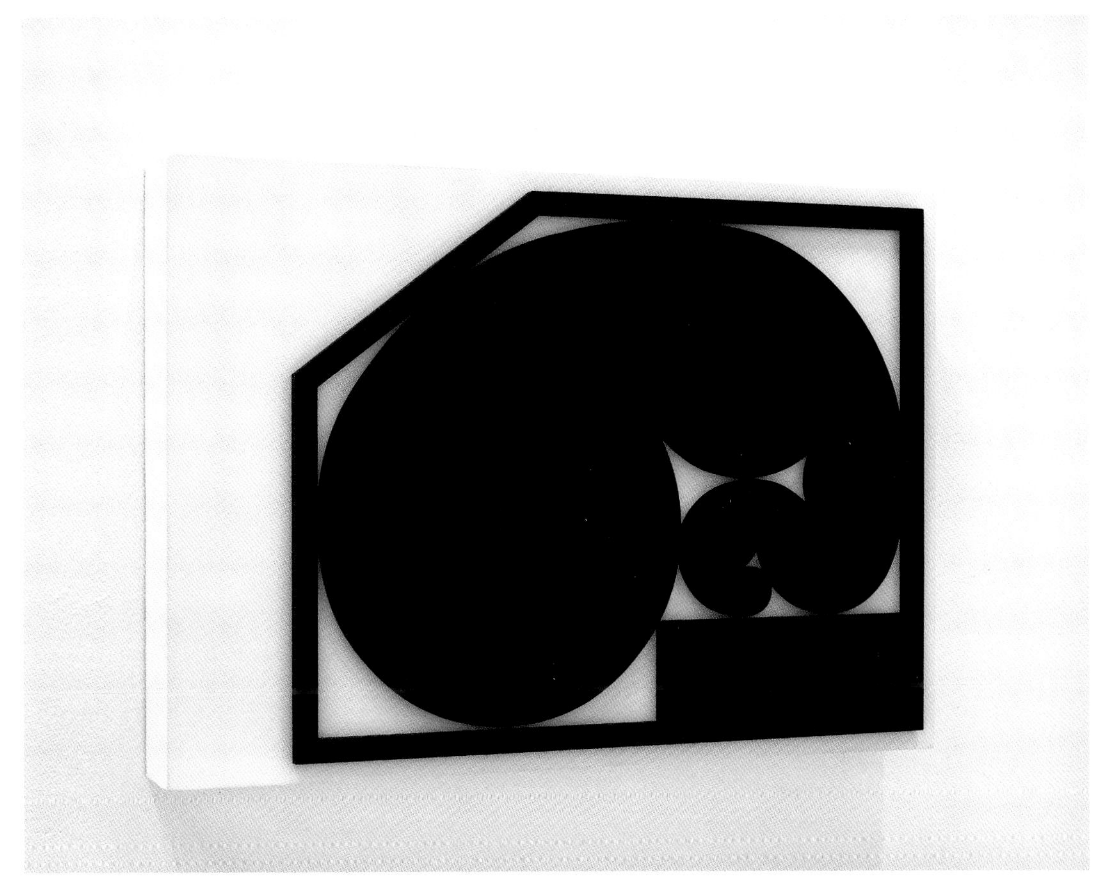

Reciprocal
MDF and acrylics
33 x 39 x 4 cm
2009

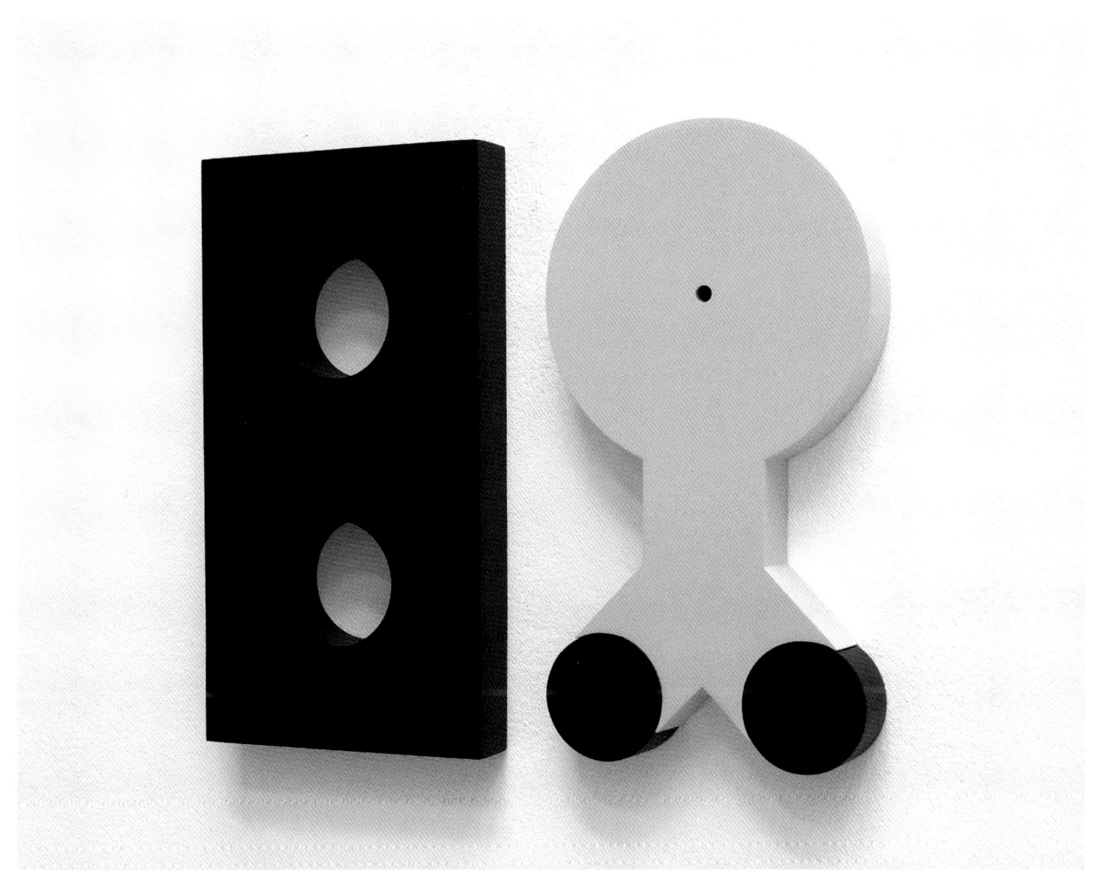

Source
Acrylics and
collage on paper
152 x 102 cm
2009

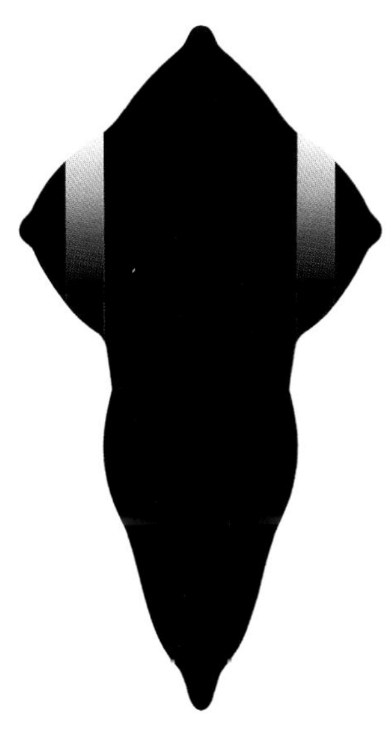

Hope
Acrylics on paper
152 x 122 cm
2009

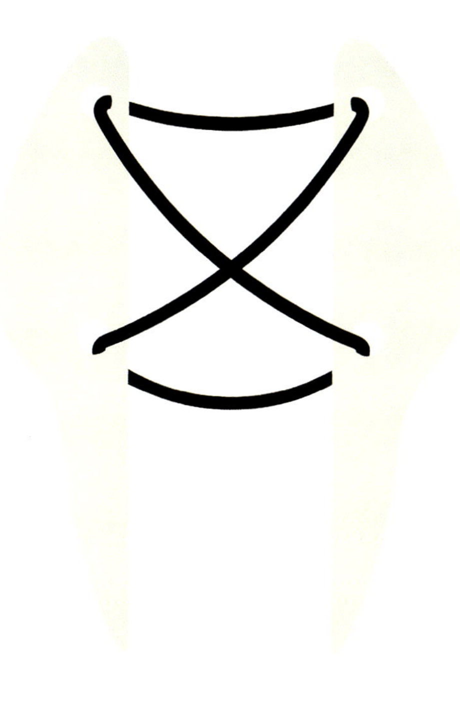

From the Woods
Acrylics on paper
152 x 122 cm
2011

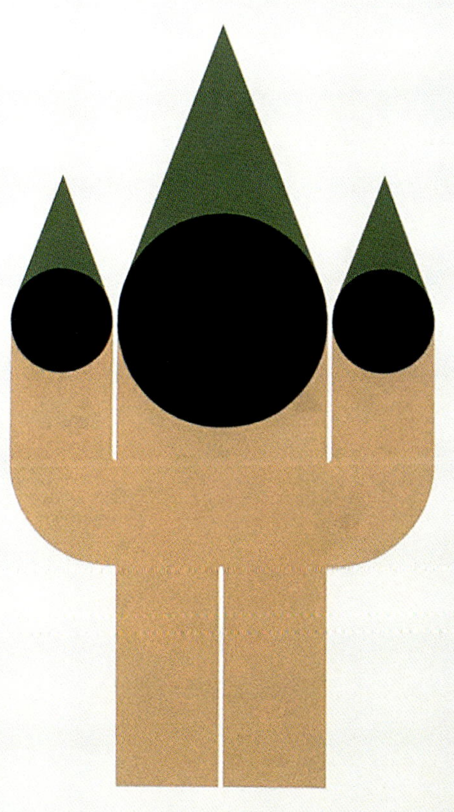

Saint
Acrylics on paper
218.44 x 139.7 cm
2011

Untitled
Acrylics and
collage on paper
218.44 x 138.7 cm
2012

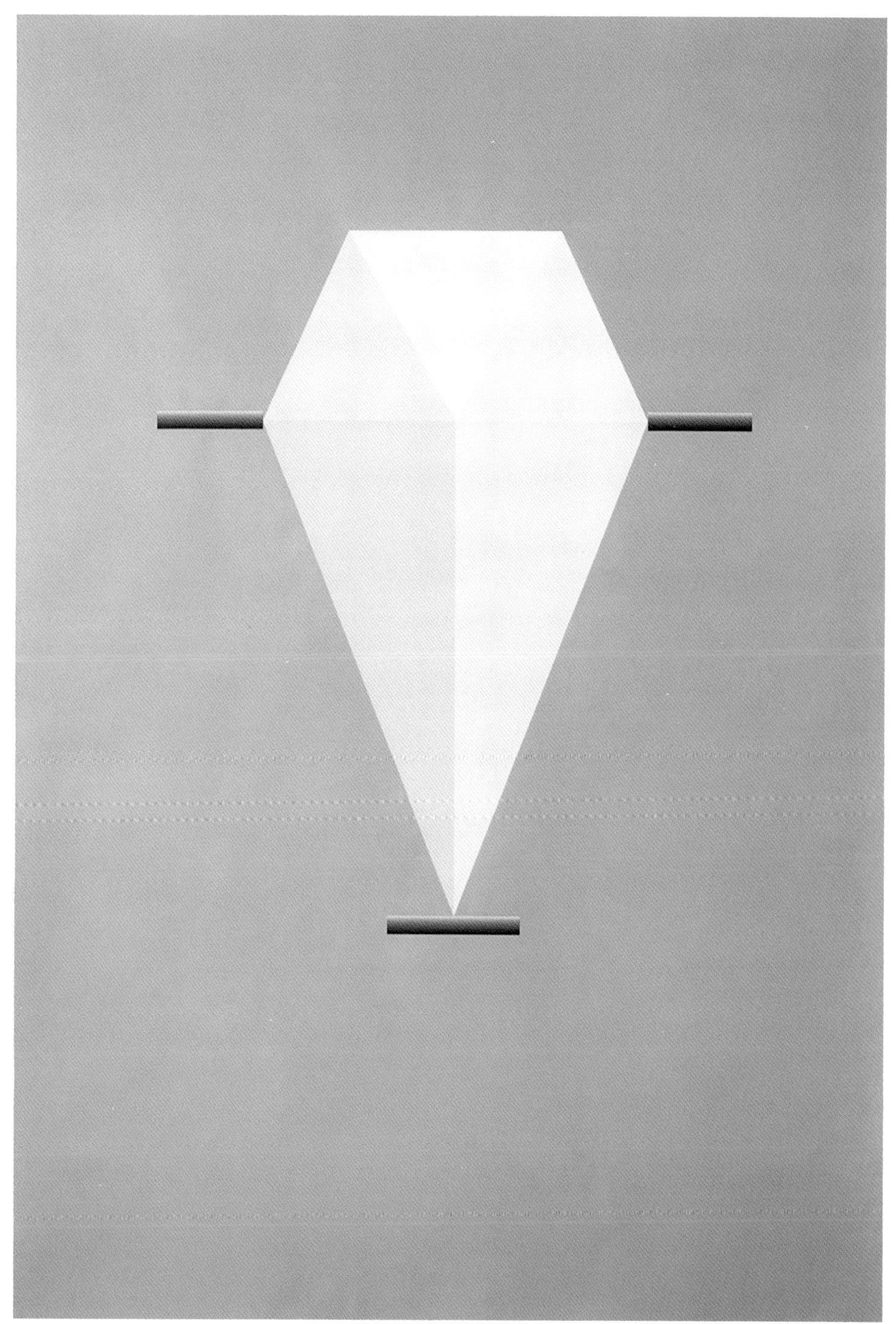

Believer
Acrylics and collage
on paper
152 x 122 cm
2012

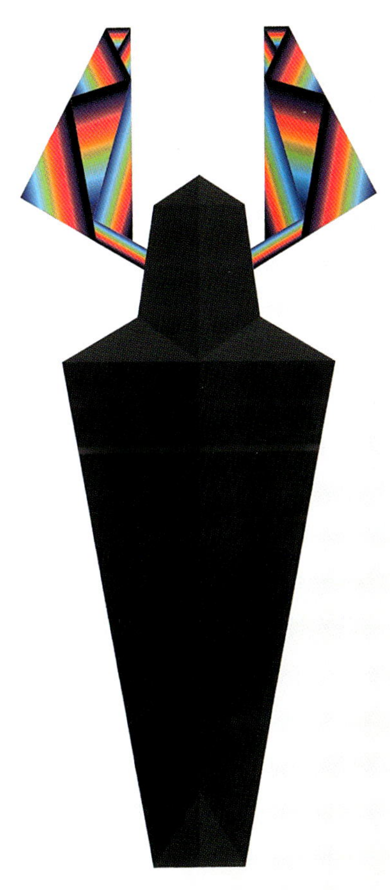

Healer
Acrylics and
collage on paper
152 x 122 cm
2012

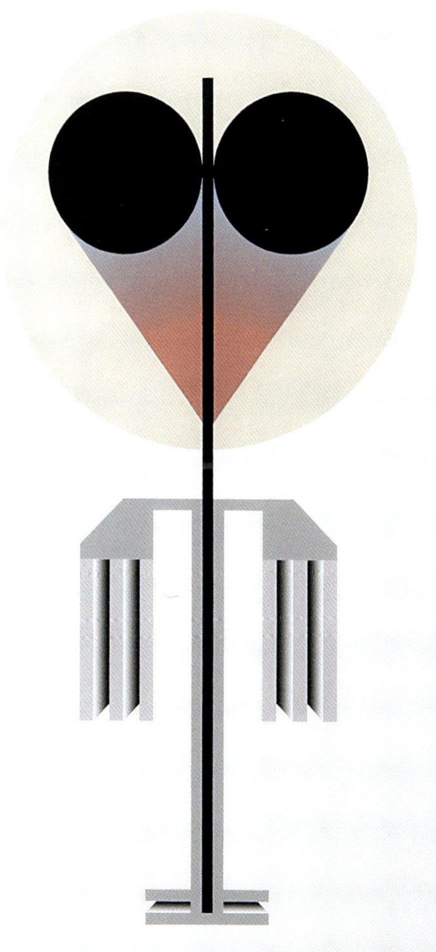

Optimist
Perspex, cedar wood
159 x 52 x 32.9 cm
2012

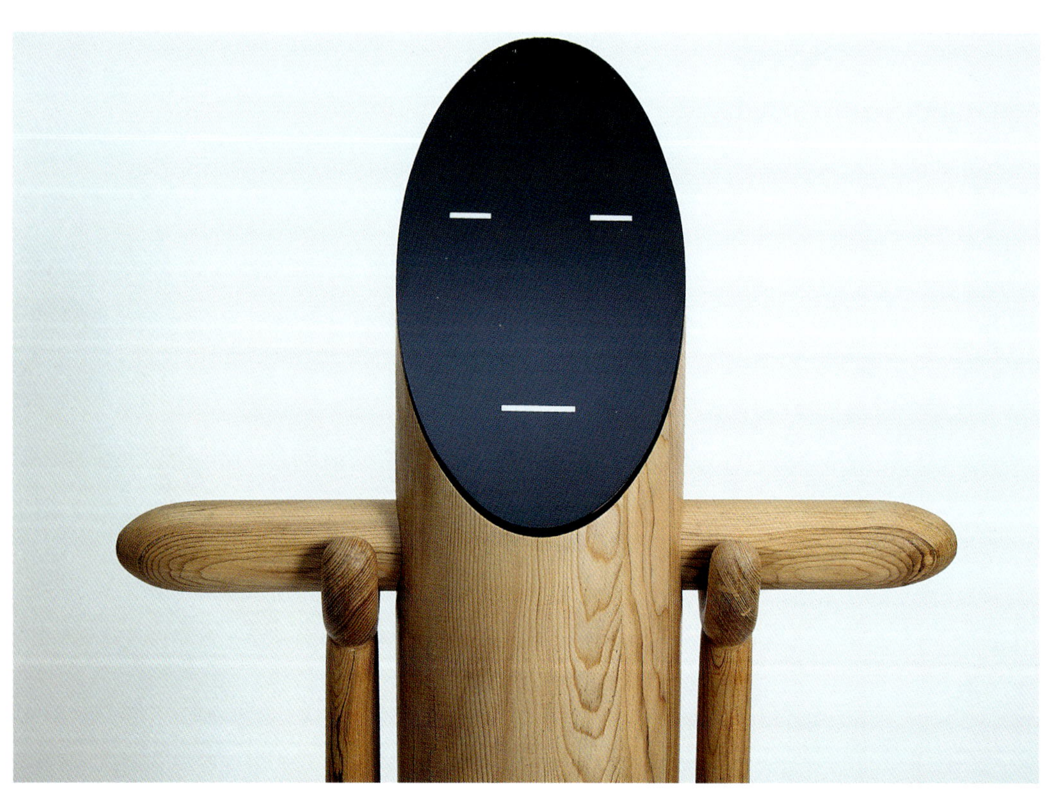

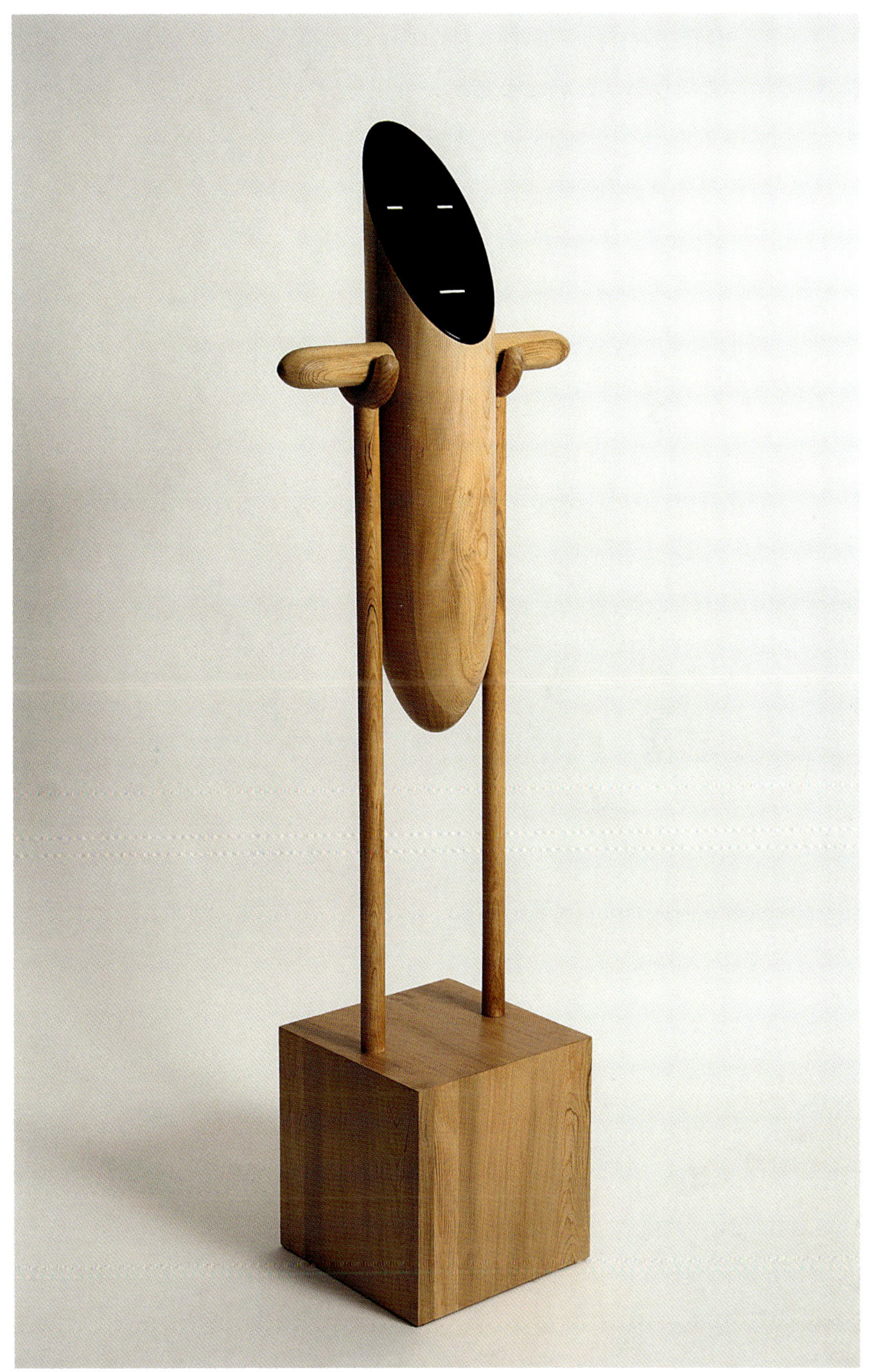

Liar
Perspex, cedar wood,
rope and iron
201.2 x 45.5 x 45.5 cm
2012

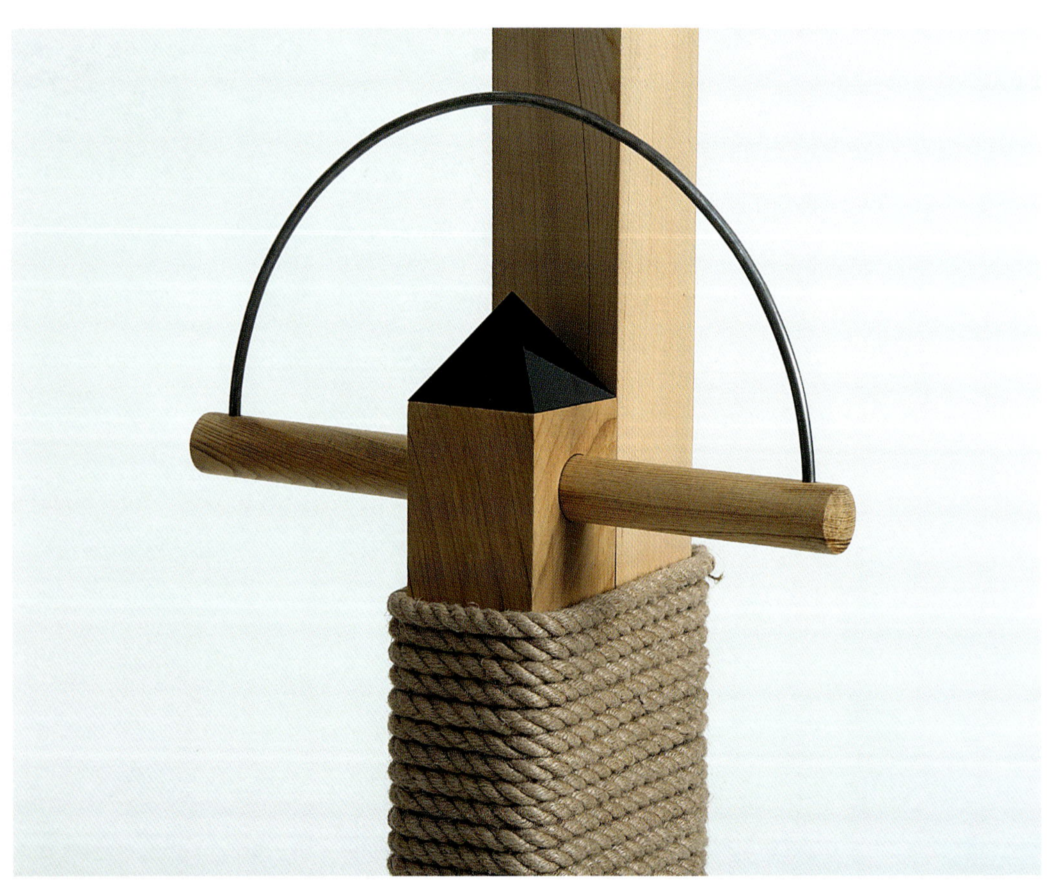

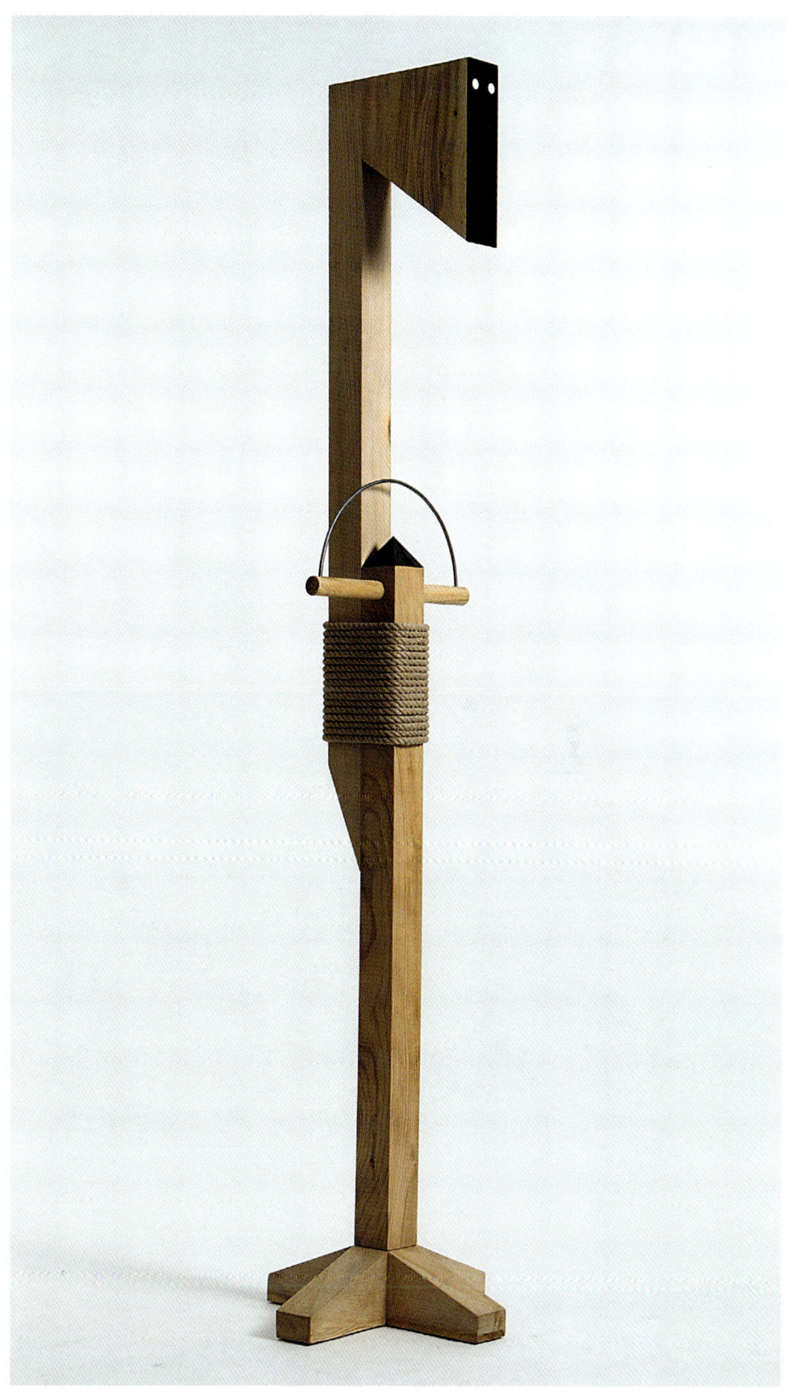

Oppressor
Charcoal on paper
76.2 x 58.42 cm
2012

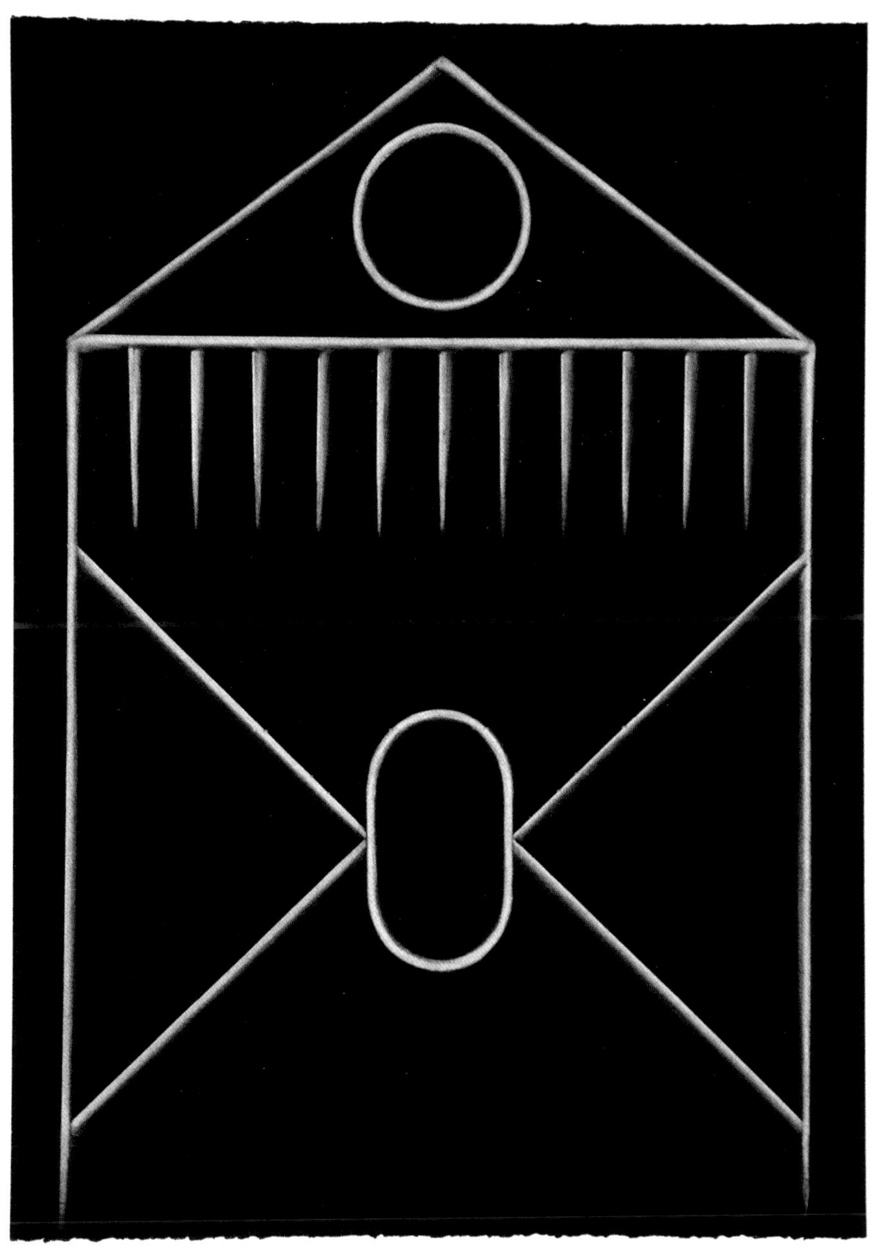

The Shape of Punishment
Acrylics on paper
51.2 x 38 cm
2012

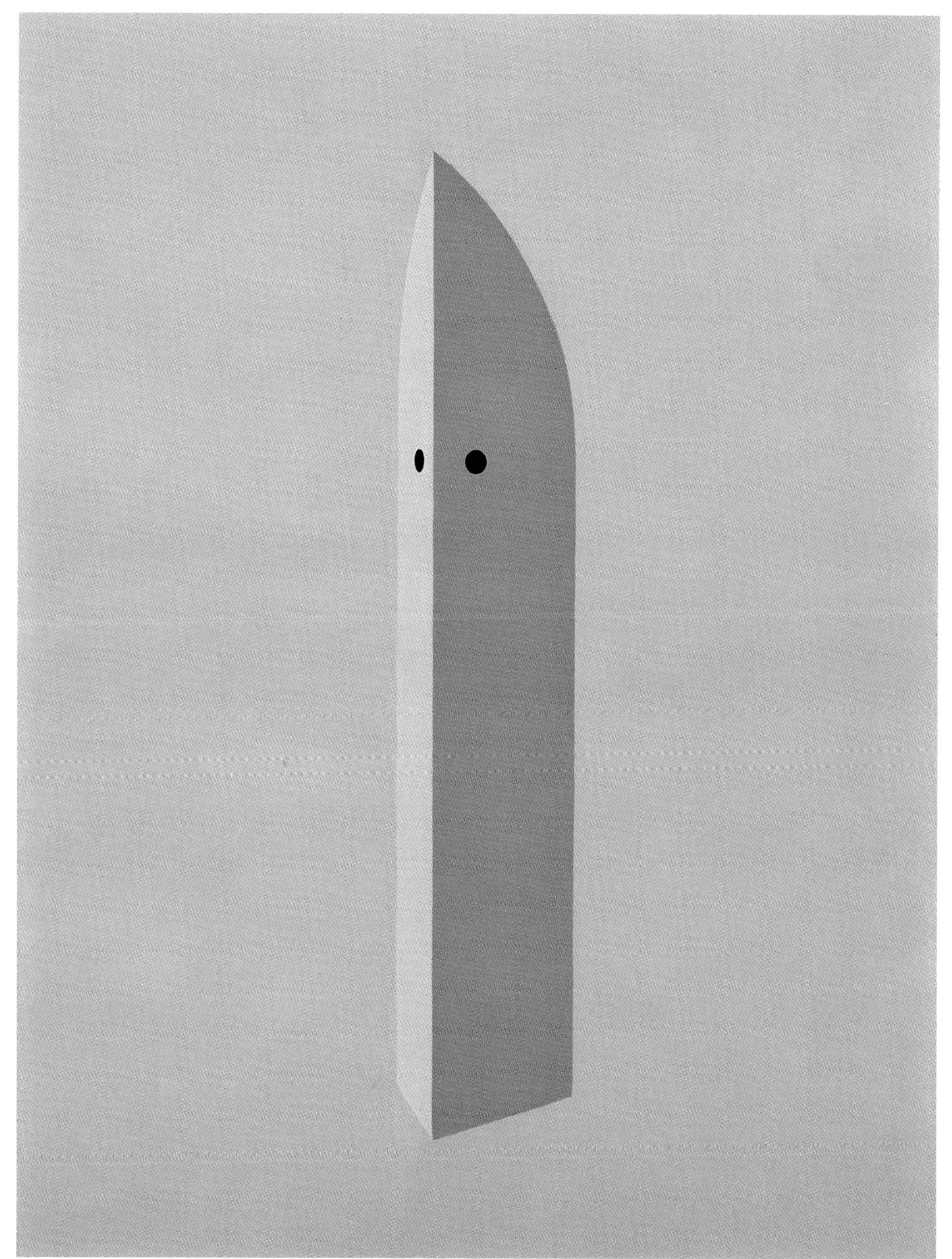

Ghost
Acrylics and pencil
on paper
52 x 38 cm
2012

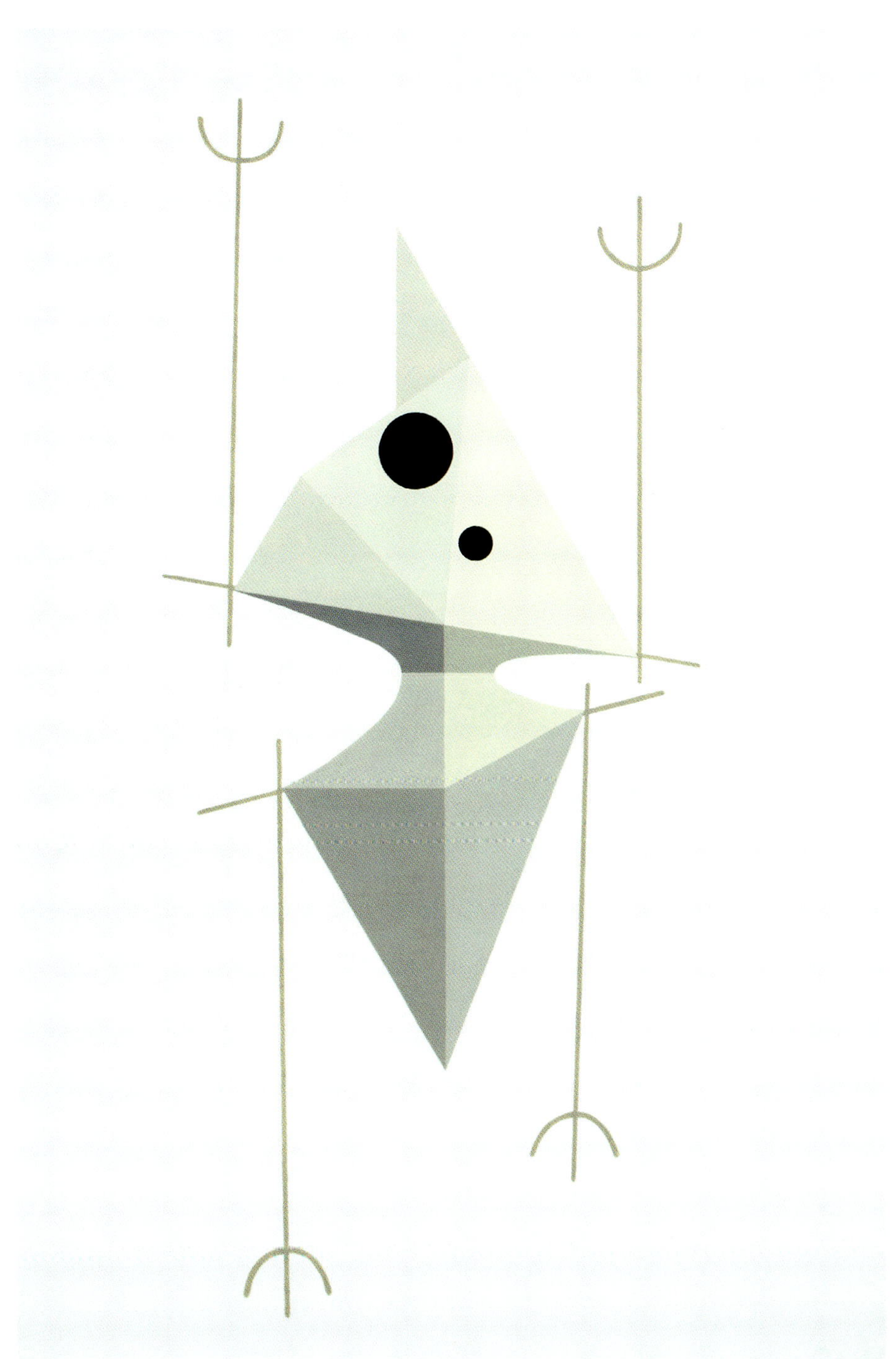

Signals
Acrylics and pencil
on paper
56.5 x 45 cm
2012

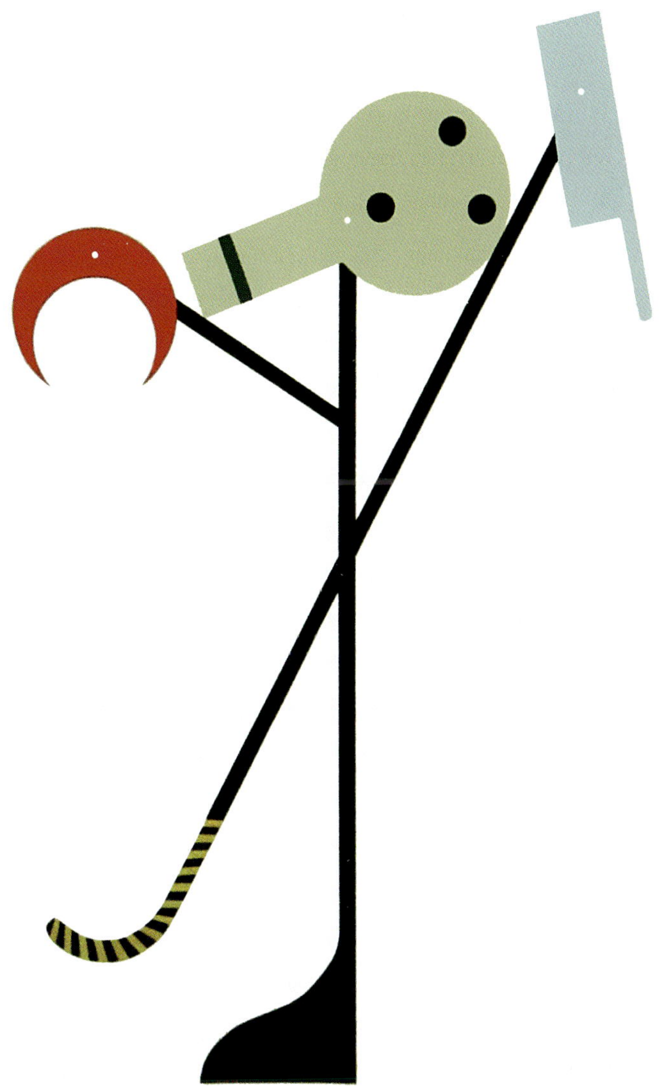

Bad Magic
Acrylics on paper
51 x 37.7 cm
2012

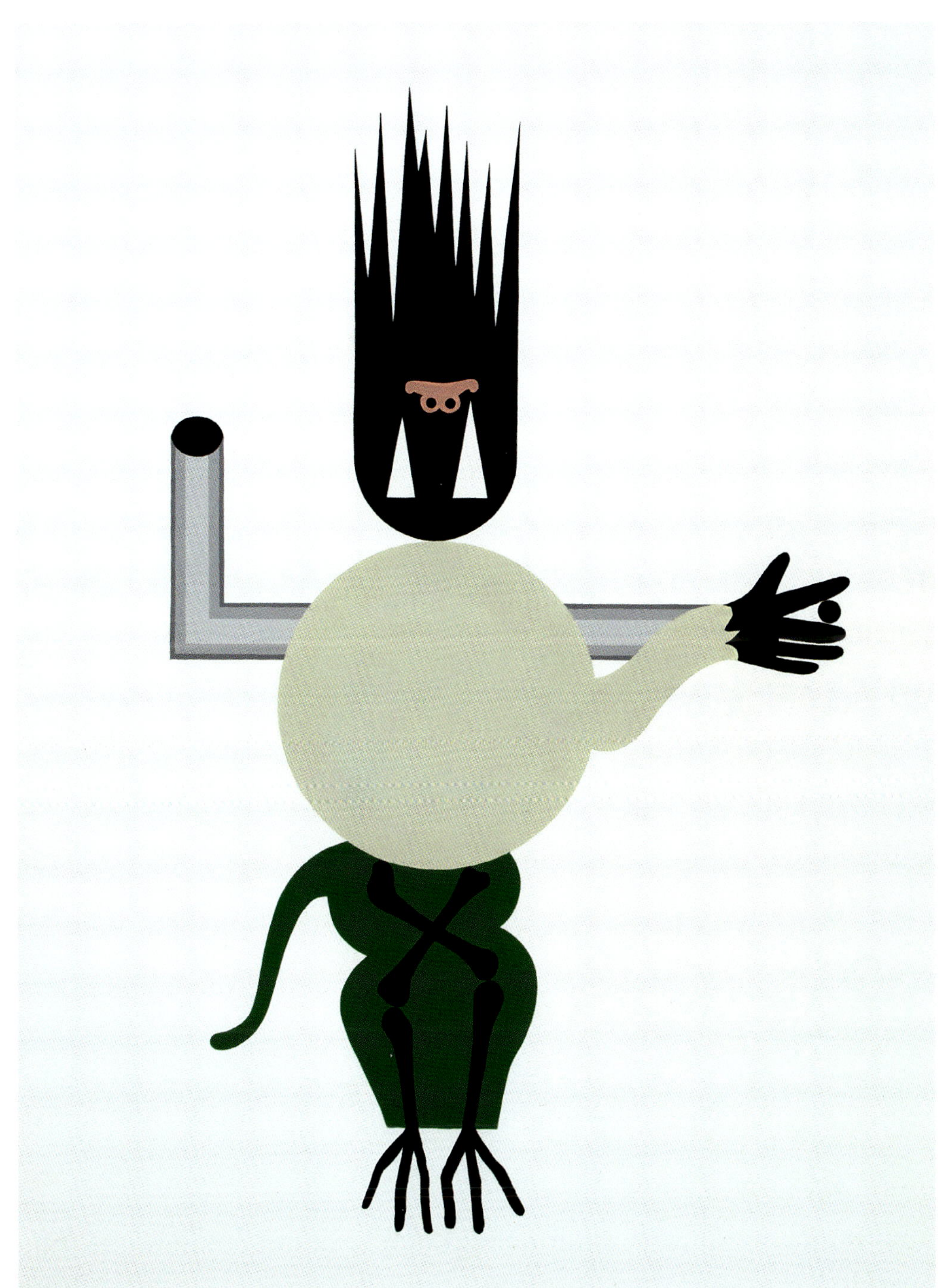

Bone Dance
Acrylics and marker
on paper
56.3 x 43.2 cm
2012

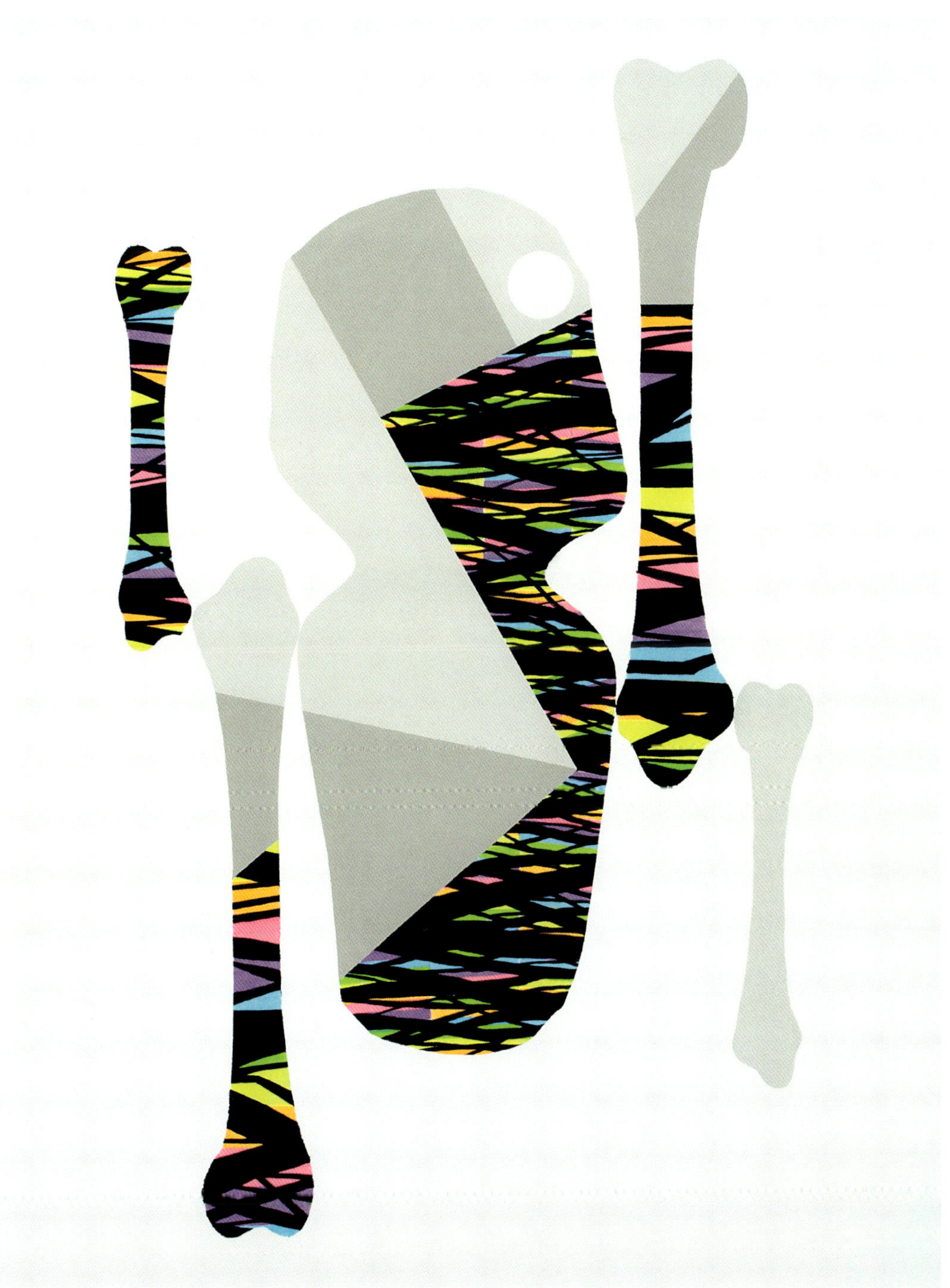

Broadcast
Acrylics and marker
on paper
48.2 x 40.5 cm
2012

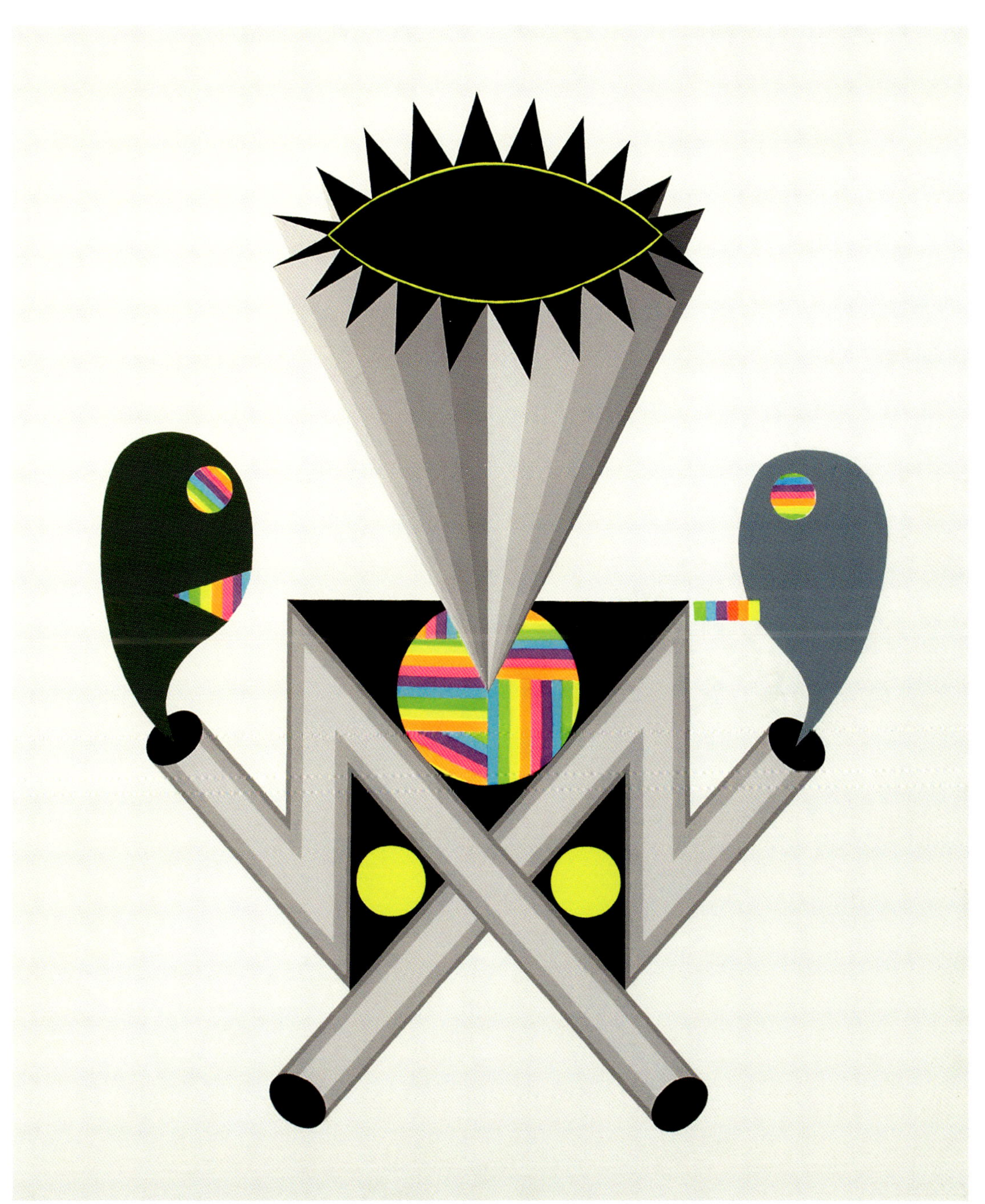

His Masters Voice
Acrylics and marker
on paper
51.5 x 37.5 cm
2012

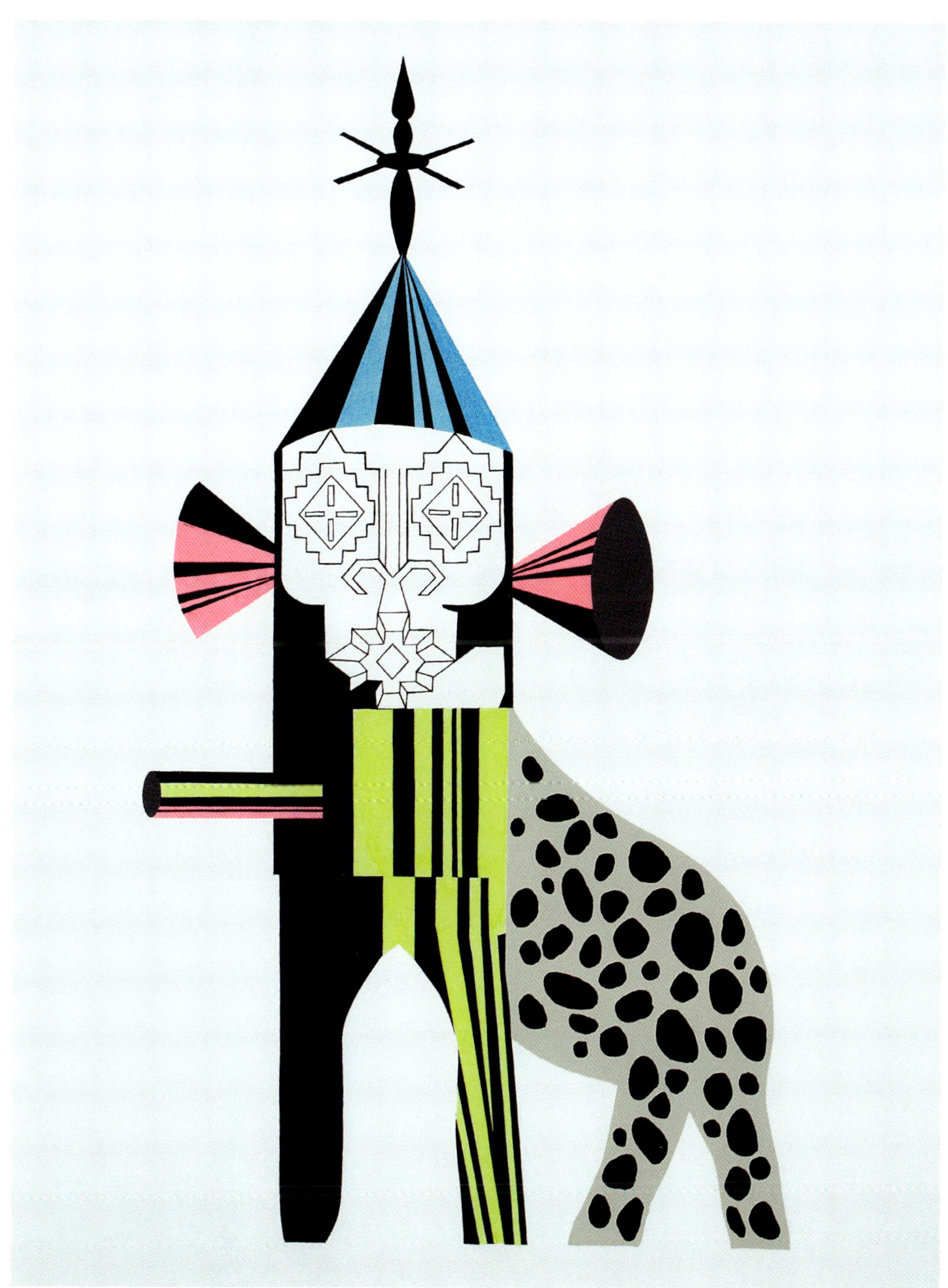

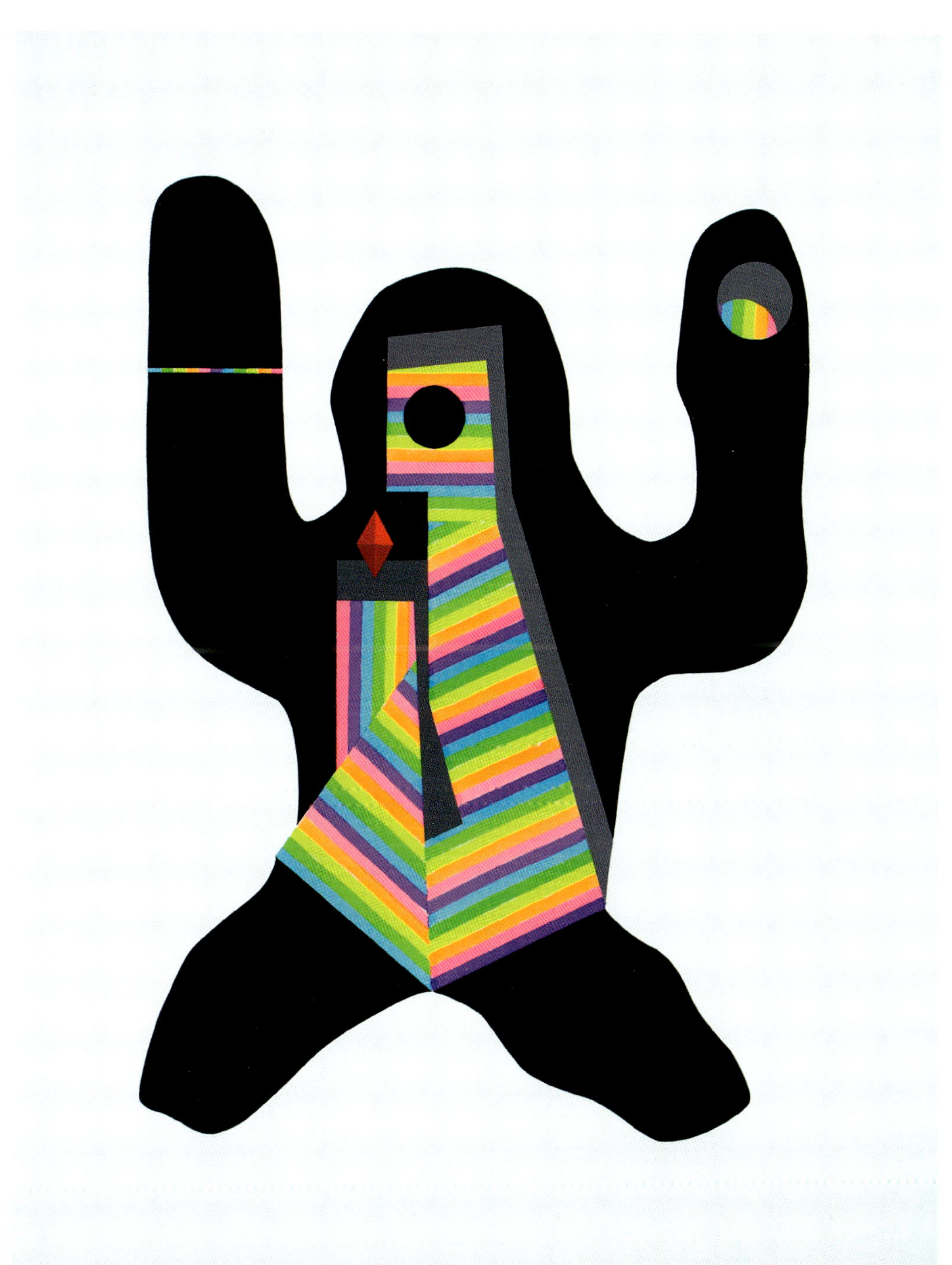

Urn
Acrylics and marker
on paper
56.5 x 43.3 cm
2012

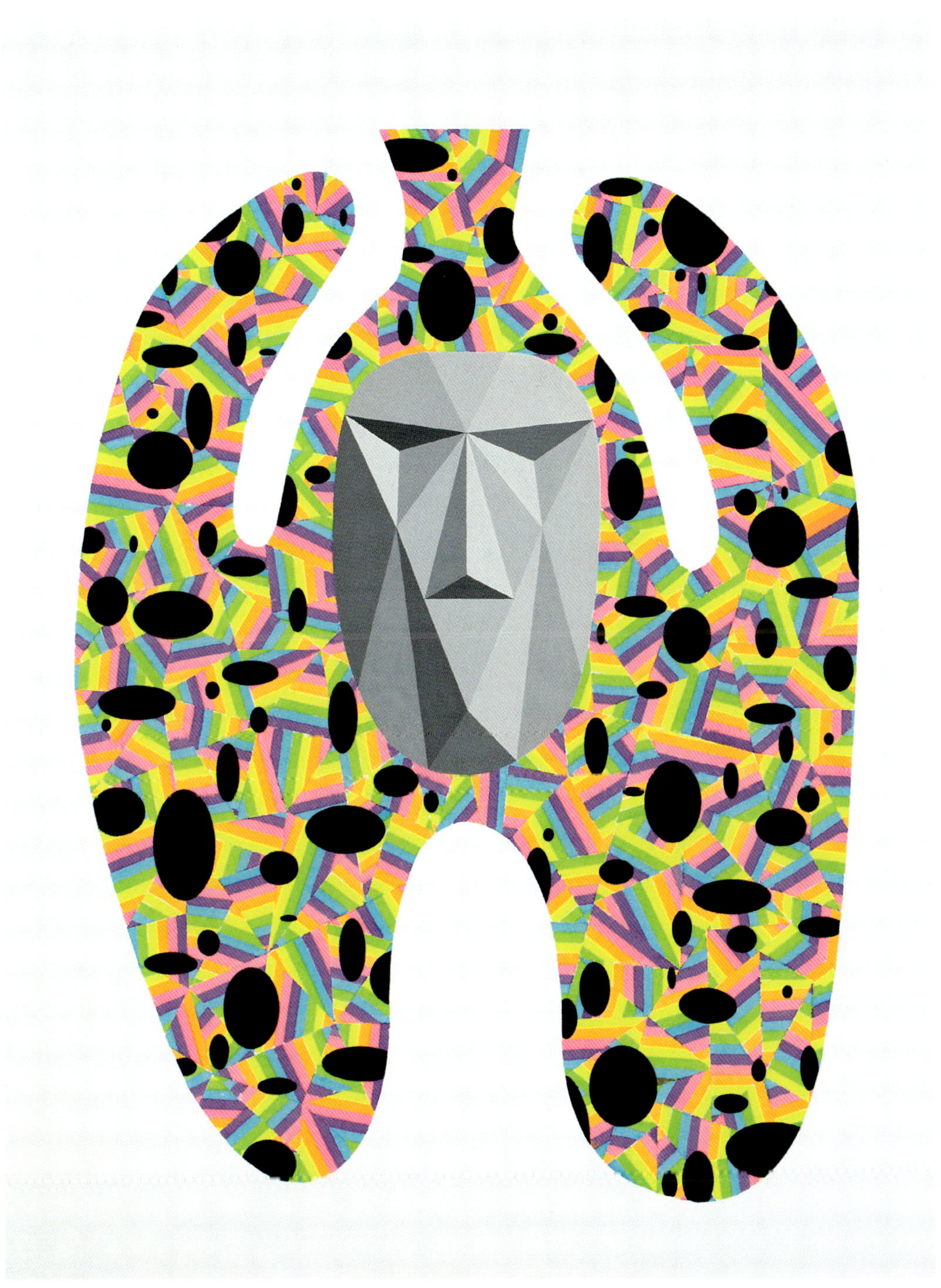

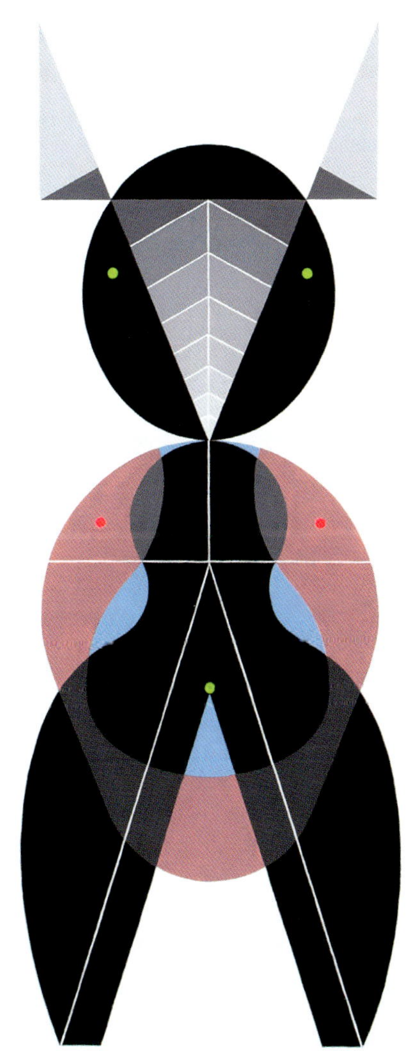

Saint Eclipse
Acrylics on paper
56 x 38 cm
2012

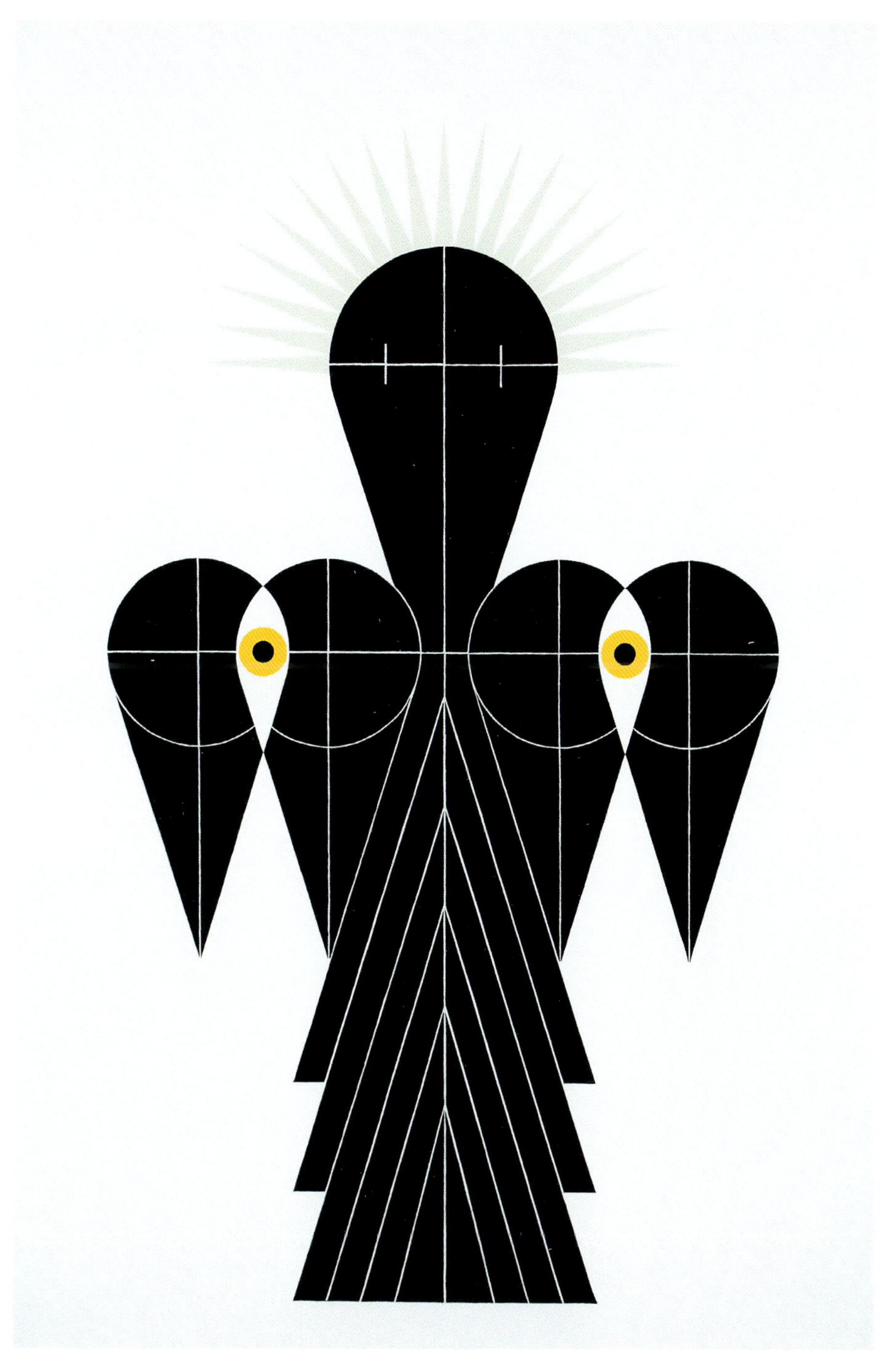

Stars at Elbow and Foot
Acrylics and
marker on paper
56.7 x 37.8 cm
2012

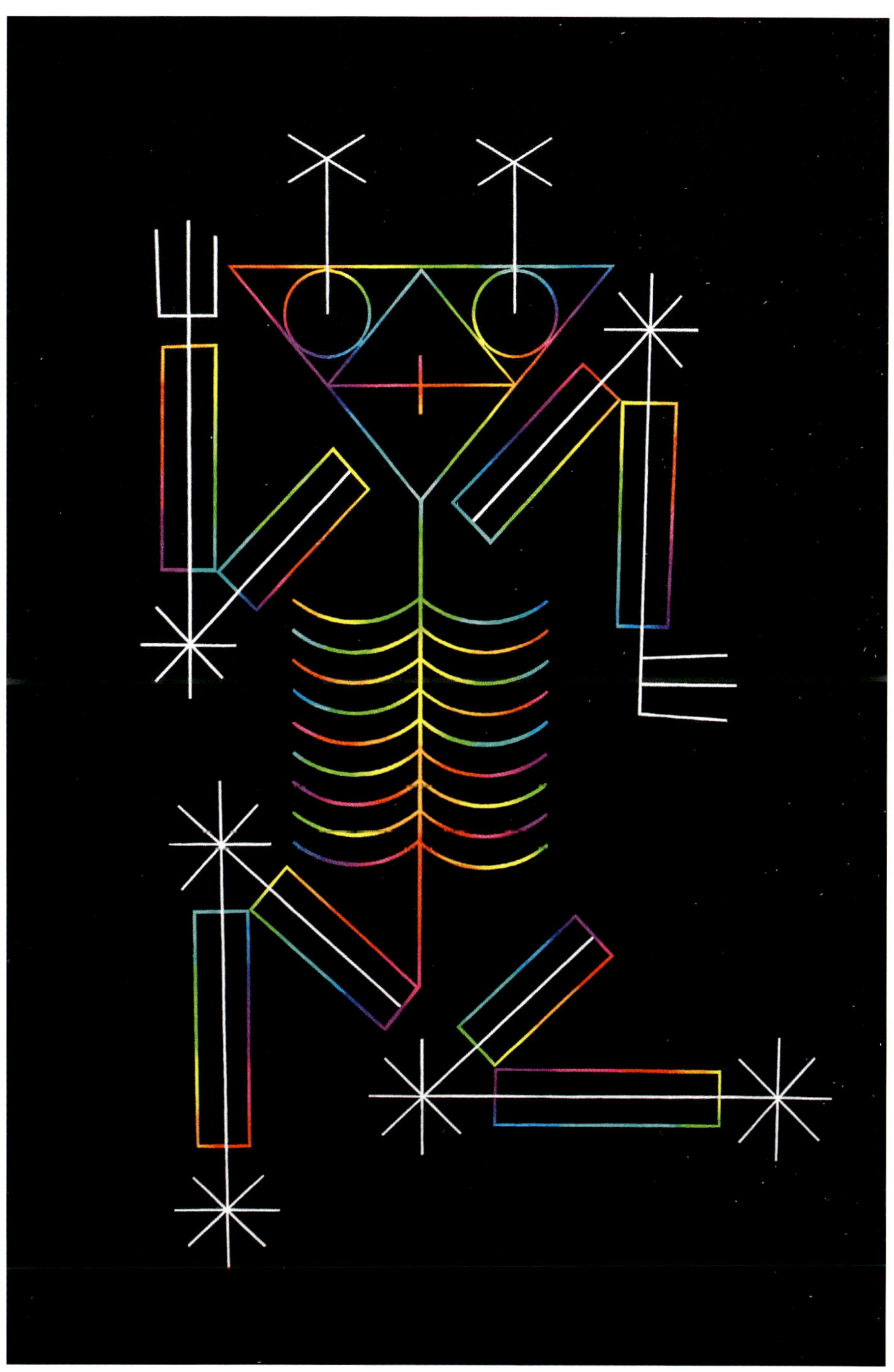

Prayer for Circuits
Acrylics and
marker on paper
57 x 43.2 cm
2012

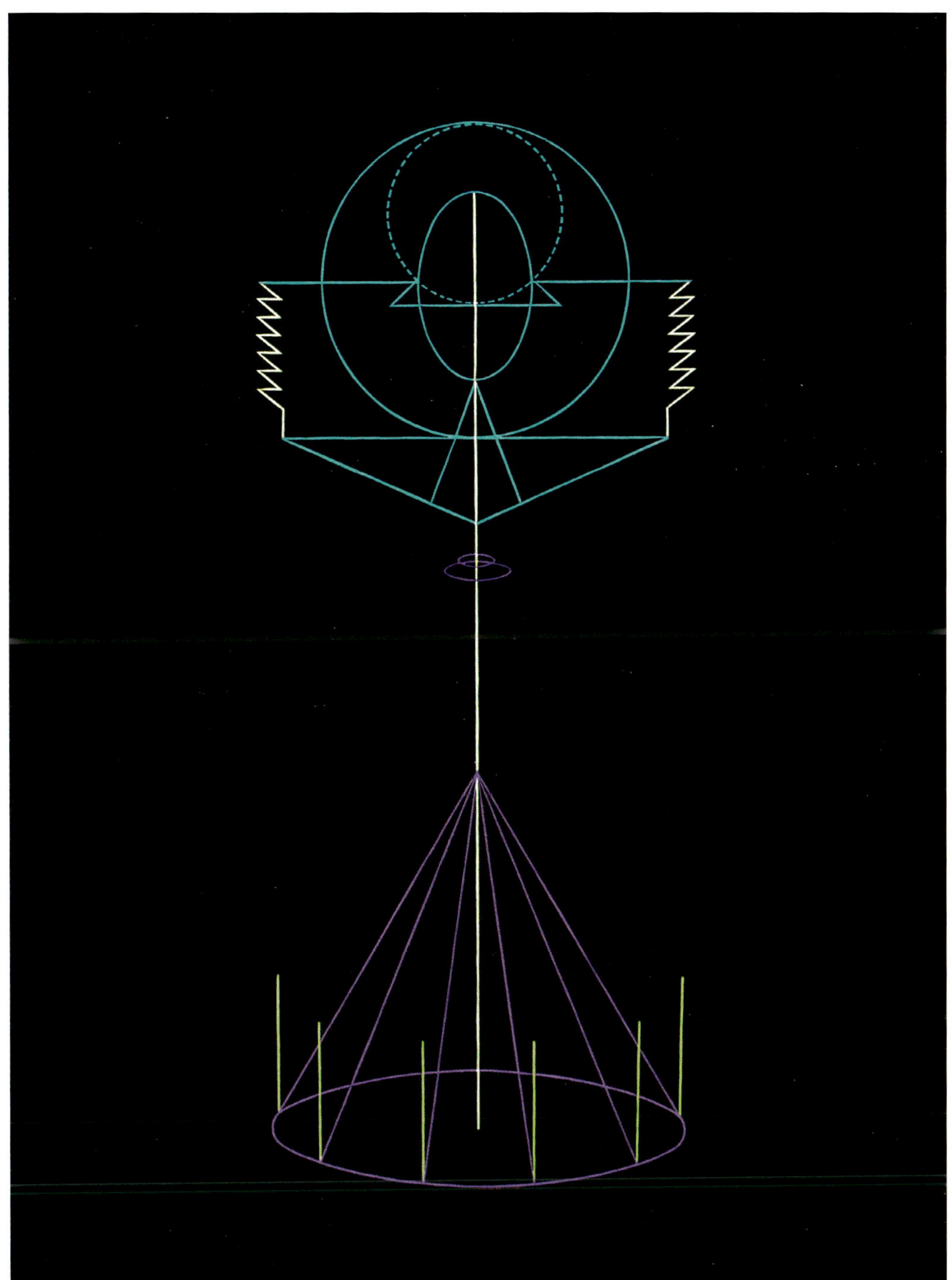

Ascent
Acrylics and
marker on paper
56.5 x 43.2 cm
2012

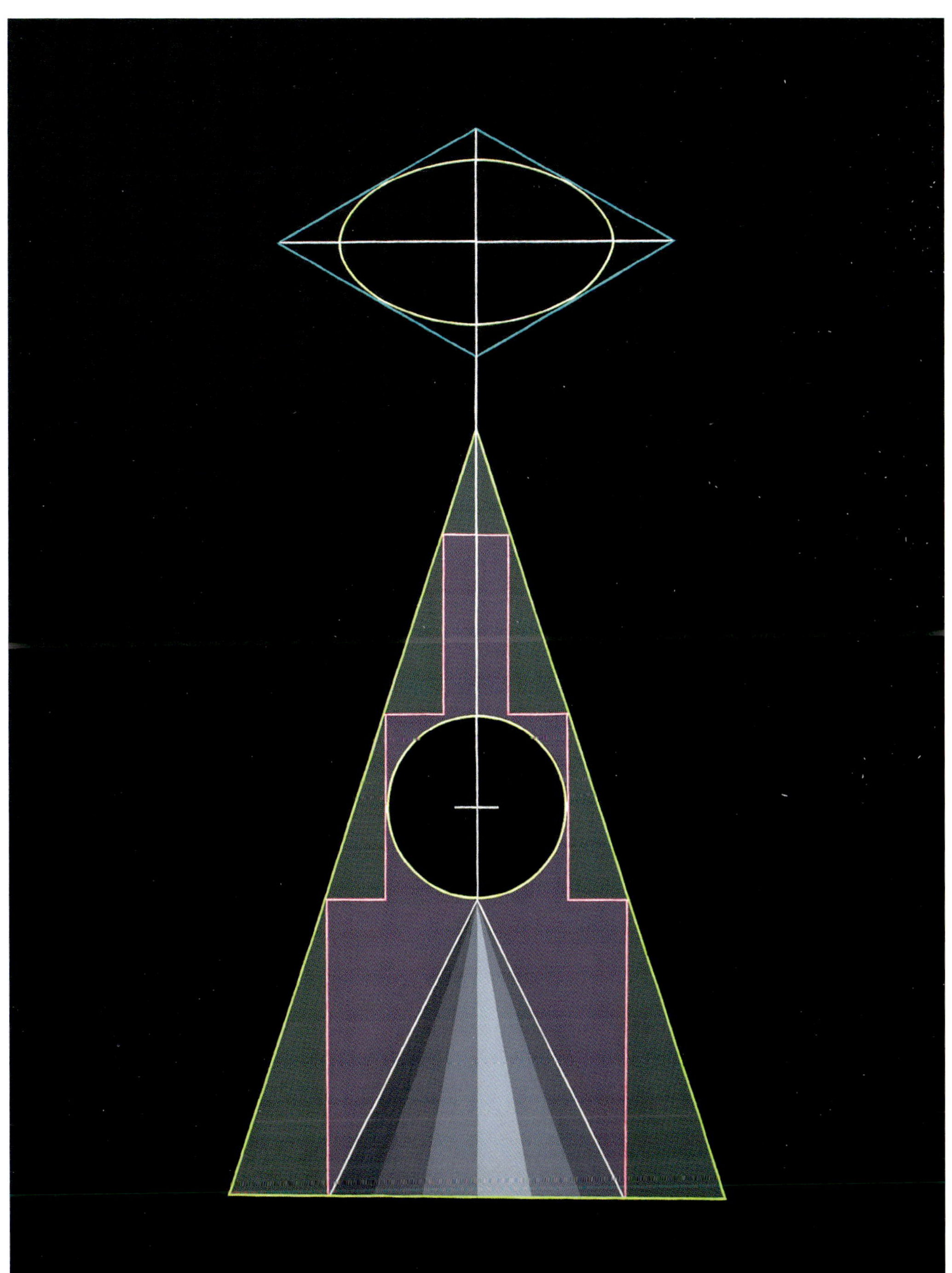

Shame
Acrylics and
marker on paper
32.4 x 38.2 cm
2012

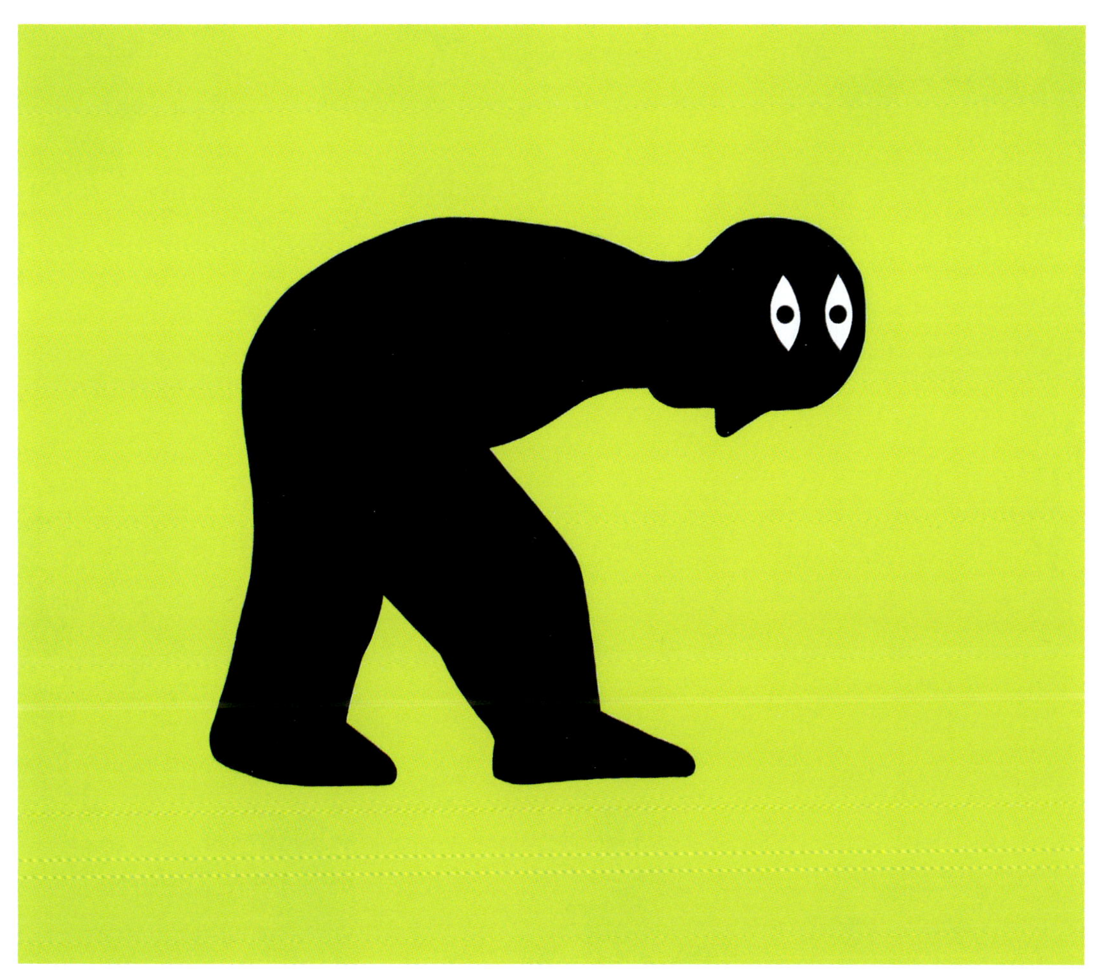

Toward Light
Screen print on paper
112.5 x 76.5 cm
Edition of 8 + 1 AP
2013

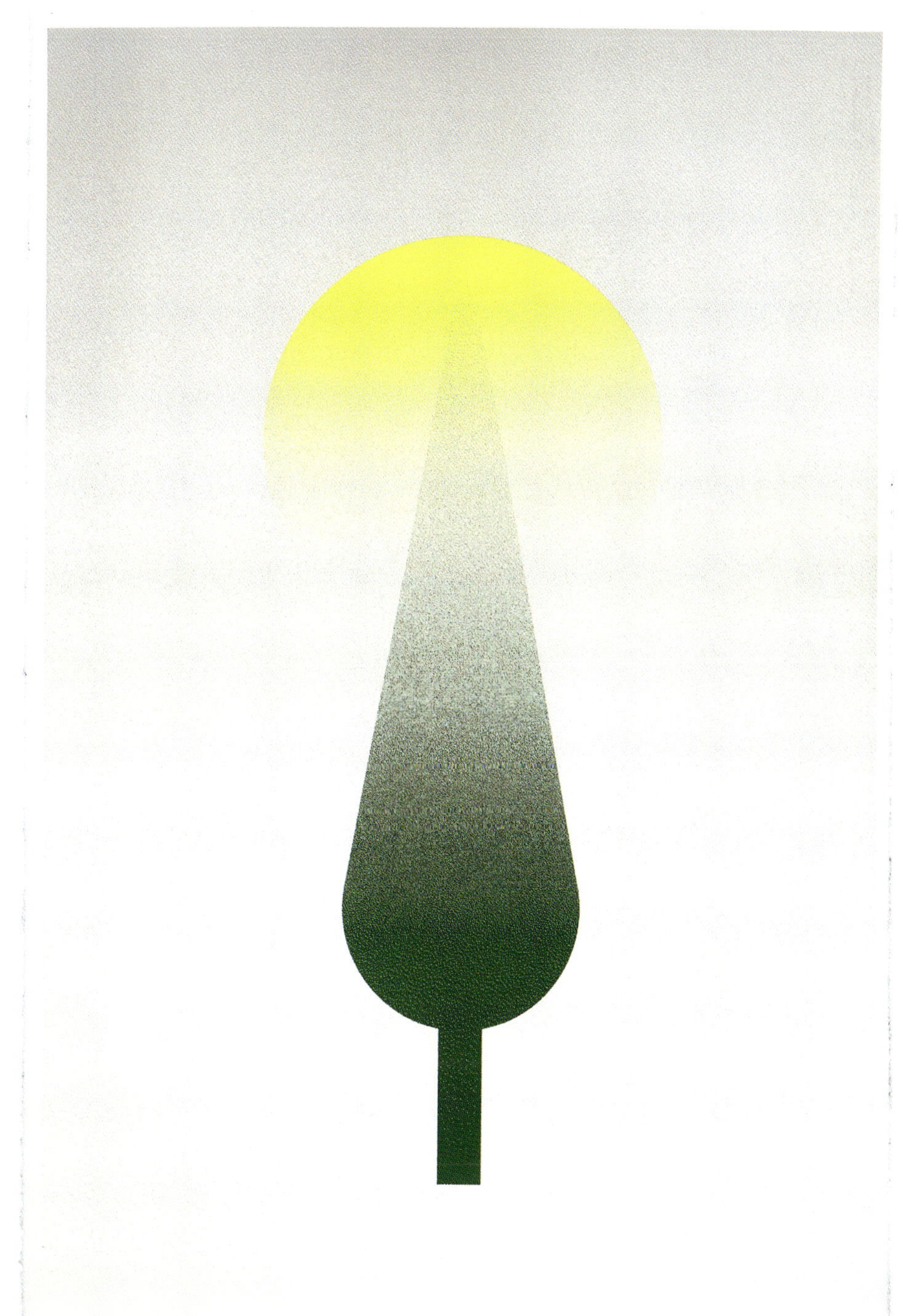

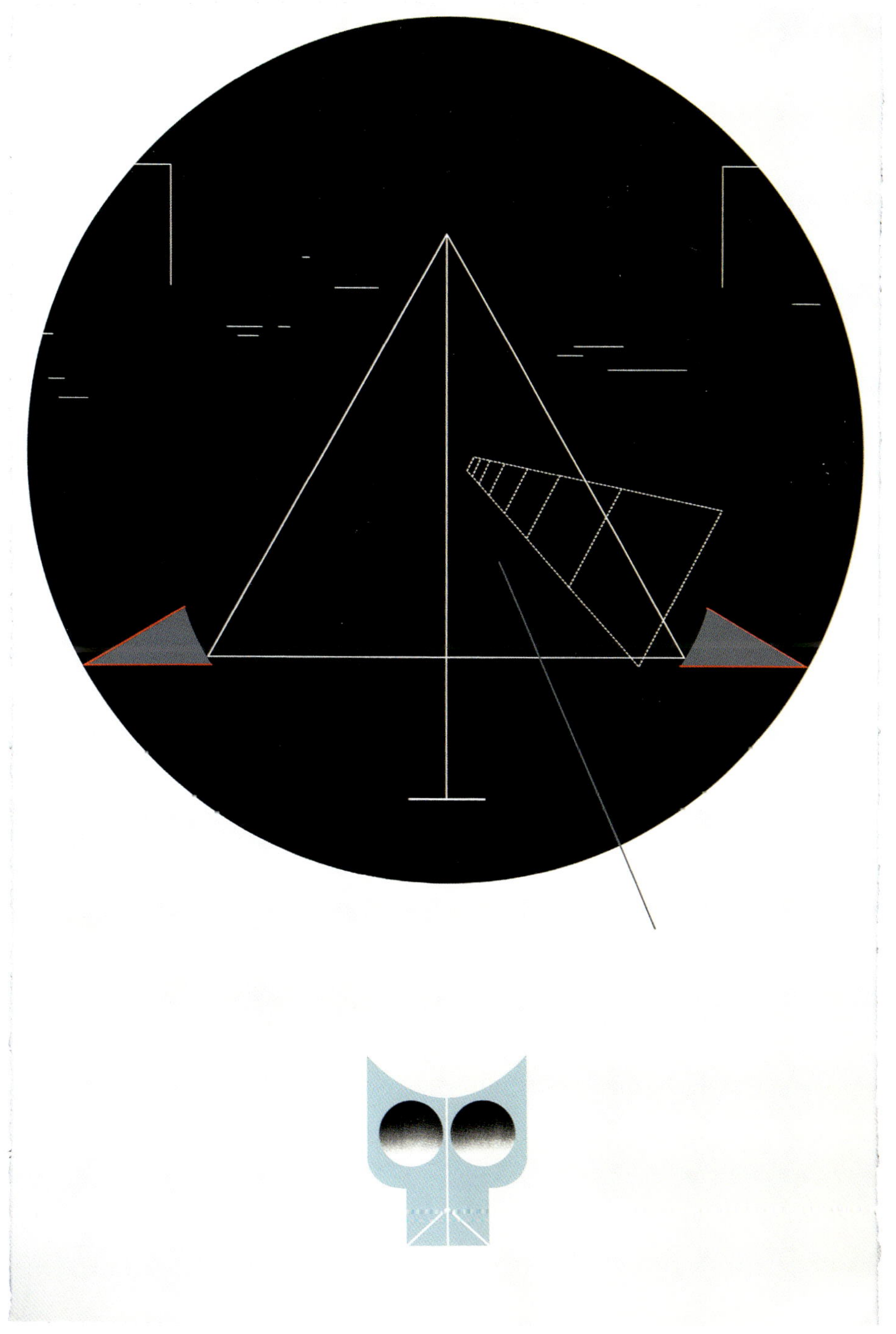

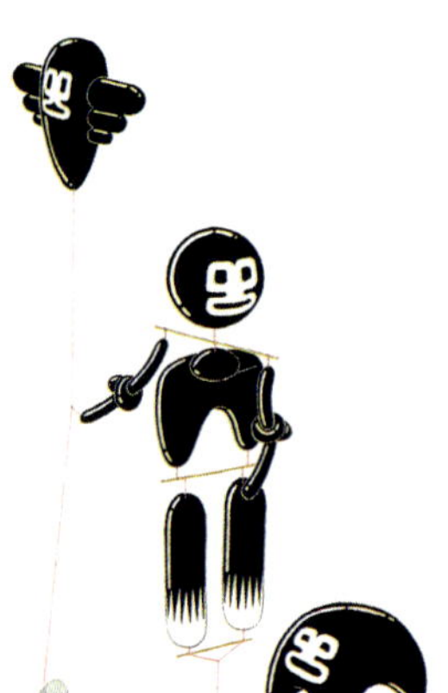

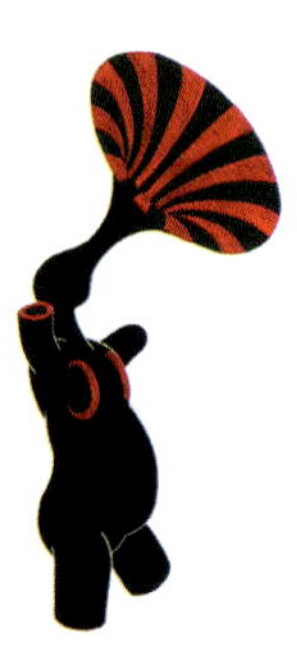

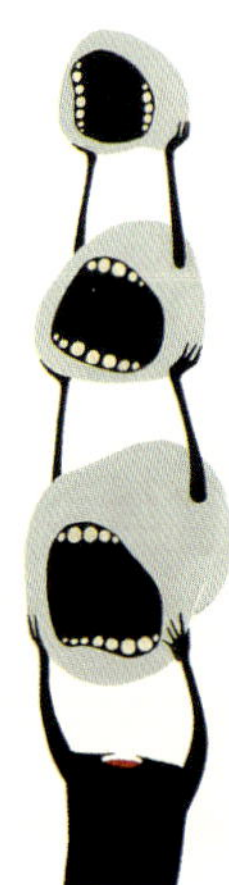

Top left
Totem, 2007

Bottom left
Siren, 2007

Bottom right
Echo, 2007

Uncertain Icons

Fahd Burki's art can leave one feeling uncertain. Though conceptually rigorous, formally exact and precisely executed, his paintings, drawings and sculptures stubbornly insist on ambiguity. They are almost impossible to place. Whether narrative scenes or flattened icons, his images often lack a background; without a specific cultural frame or spatial context to help locate them, they hover in an atopia or, rather, a dystopia of infinite reference, outside of time and history. Archaic iconography and visions of the future comfortably coexist in these works and profound 'dys-chrony' pulses through them. Though undeniably contemporary, they also feel anachronistic and untimely, resolutely not of the now. But as Italian philosopher Giorgio Agamben suggests, this quality, of being both in and out of sync with the present, is precisely a part of being contemporary.[1] Burki draws on sources that span various histories, geographies and cultures including the mythologies and iconographies of aboriginal and indigenous cultures, especially Native American, ukiyo-e prints and manga from Japan, Eastern European animation, science fiction, and other strands of contemporary popular culture. These disparate visual and literary sources are moulded through theories, concepts and terms borrowed from anthropology and archaeology, mythology and folklore, existentialism and psychoanalysis. Combining, manipulating and transforming these varied sources, Burki makes them entirely his own, creating images that exude formal conviction but resist easy reading. His enigmatic images could be understood as contemporary manifestations of the Jungian archetypes that populate the collective unconscious.

Take *Totem* (2007), a small curious painting in acrylic on paper, in which a Native American totem pole appears to have disassembled into its various components.[2] Instead of stacked and packed into a weighty monumental column, the individual totems float free like balloons. Barely held together by a delicate armature, the parts of the largest one resemble an inverted mobile. The unexpected whimsy of the scene opens its iconography up to more contemporary readings; simplified, stylised and repeated, the mask-like faces of the totems begin to remind us of both cartoon characters and the hoods worn by the heroes and villains of 'lucha libre'.[3] *Totem* is an early work, one of a series of paintings Burki exhibited together under the title "Cult of Man", a reference, possibly, to Émile Durkheim's theory on how religion's social function might evolve in an increasingly individualistic modern society. Like isolated pages from an illustrated book, each work in the series presents a distinct tableau within a blank field. Literally ungrounded, the scenes float like dreams through the unconscious, unfolding in a time and space of pure imagination. The various protagonists encountered – anthropomorphic but not entirely human – are rendered as opaque patches of flatly applied acrylic paint with minimal, if any, shading. And while they have limbs and, hence, remain capable of action, they are often acephalic, lacking precisely that part of the body that is the locus of identity, subjectivity, thought, consciousness and vision. This allows the creatures to simultaneously function as universal types, and allows them to access impulses and drives and engage in actions that lie outside reason.[4]

1. Giorgio Agamben, "What Is the Contemporary?", in *What Is an Apparatus? And Other Essays*, transl. by David Kishik and Stefan Pedatella (Stanford: Stanford University Press, 2009), pp. 39–54.
2. Burki's use of paper as support and his interest in image as illustration was inspired, somewhat unexpectedly given his imagery, from his exposure to and study of the tradition of miniature painting in South Asia. Fahd Burki in conversation with the author, 5 October 2013.
3. Roland Barthes drew a comparable link between mythology and popular wrestling in "The World of Wrestling", in *Mythologies*, transl. by Annette Lavers (New York: Hill & Wang, 1972), pp. 15–25.
4. Derived from the Greek and meaning headless, *Acéphale* was the name of a journal and a secret society founded by the Surrealist writer Georges Bataille, who drew on the archaic, primitive, mythic and irrational as ways of transgressing convention. The cover of the journal's first issue featured a drawing by André Masson of a decapitated man who resembled Leonardo da Vinci's *Vitruvian Man*, an embodiment of classical reason.

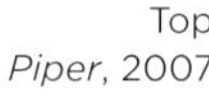

Top
Piper, 2007

Bottom
Augur, 2009

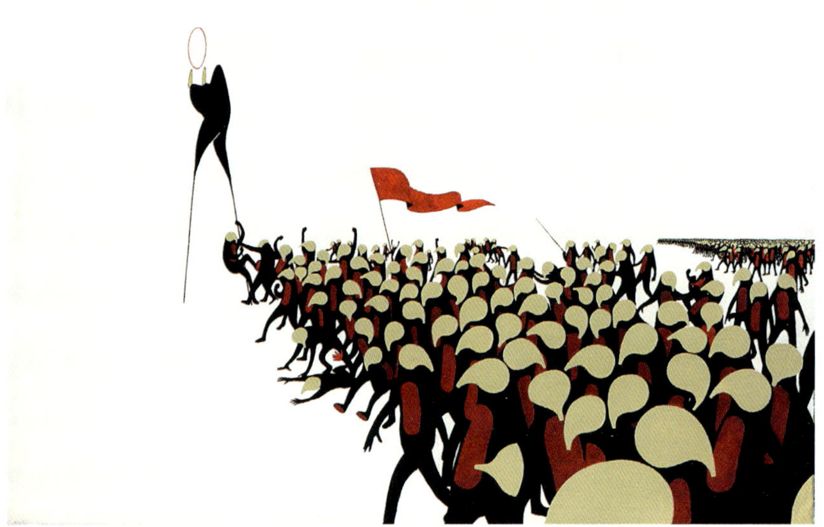

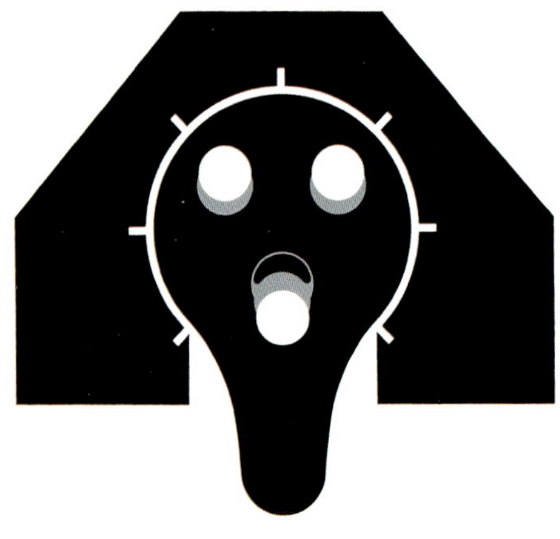

Though this series never coheres into a single narrative, some motifs are repeated. Sound or music appear embodied. In *Siren* (2007), the horn of a phonograph replaces the head of a figure whose arms and legs, though reduced to stumps, extend as if in midstride. In *Echo* (2007), a torso holds its eyeless head aloft, its mouth open wide; arms emerging from this head hold up a similar but smaller head, which repeats the gesture one more time. The image wittily illustrates the repetition and diminishing intensity that characterise an echo. And musical instruments – a horn, a cymbal and a pair of ghungroos – and players fuse together in *Revelers* (2007, page 31). Similarly, subtle references to masquerades and play appear in *Troupe* (2007, pages 32–33) and *Reverie* (2007, page 41), emphasised through their titles. Burki's interest in theatricality stems from its central role in ritual practices like shamanism, in which the sacred may only be accessed through performance. In works like *Ritual* (2007, page 59) and *Altars* (2007, page 39) religious artefacts come alive and enact esoteric rites. These various strands seem to congeal in *Piper* (2007), in which a headless figure, cloaked in black and elevated on stilts, leads a mass of followers. While an oracular oval hovering above outstretched hands stands in for the piper's head, the bodies of the clamouring hordes are all topped by golden commas: though the piper might claim clairvoyance, all the figures lack the faculty of sight, and the image warns of the danger of the blind leading the blind.

Since 2009, Burki's work has begun to display a strong graphic quality, adopting the clear, precise syntax of signs and logos. Assertive, enigmatic and multivalent, these new age icons retain some of the mysterious aura of their religious predecessors, both pagan and Christian. A single image – flat, frontal and floating against an even background – dominates each frame. Composed of sharply edged geometric forms and lines that mimic the cold neutrality of a digital image, each carefully calibrated work is precisely and somewhat perversely executed by hand, using matte acrylic paints (with occasional collage elements) on paper, in a suitably sober, almost drab, palette of black, taupe, and a series of chalky greys and pasty pinks. These works demonstrate a pronounced move towards abstraction, not just as a formal endpoint but as a process, a rigorous and reductive analytical method used to arrive at a stubbornly ambivalent image, one that consciously tests the very limits of signification and narrativization; that probes precisely how little information is required for an image to remain legible. Rather than limiting meaning, this methodology paradoxically exaggerates the arbitrariness of the semiotic sign. Abstraction, both formal and semiotic, pushes the sign beyond the traditional relation of signifier and signified, opening it up to hold and receive the intangible – those ideas, affects and experiences that might escape reason, language and representation.

The reticent simplicity of these works engages both our eyes and our curiosity, while their rigorously maintained neutrality allows them to remain semantically flexible, forcing us to use our imagination and project our interpretations onto the images.

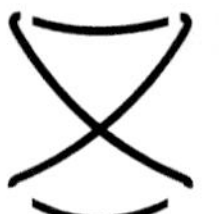

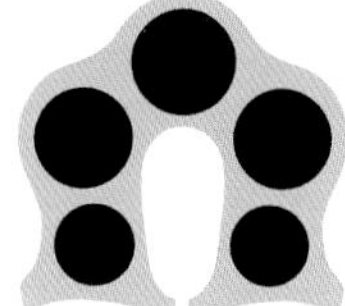

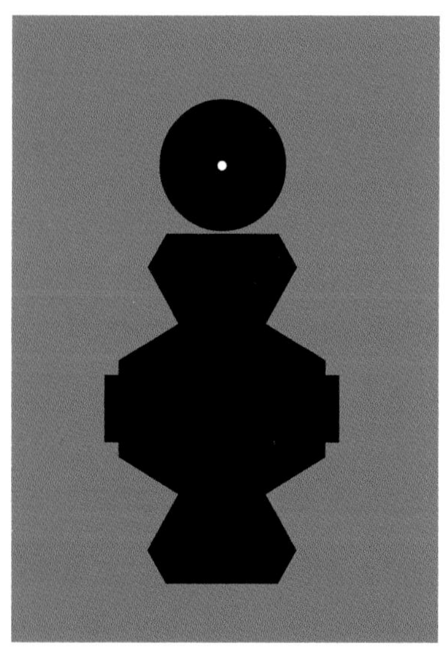

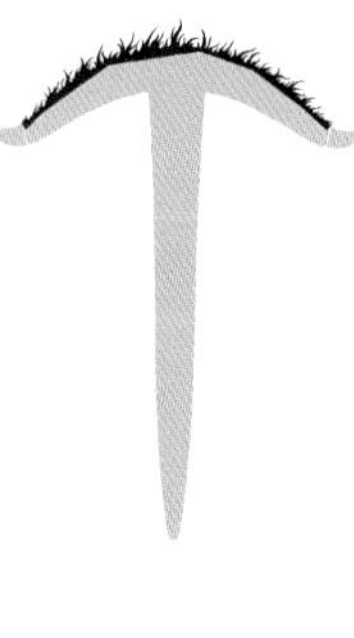

Top left
Hope, 2009

Top right
Plenitude, 2010

Bottom left
Watcher, 2010

Bottom right
Lullaby, 2010

Augur (2009) – a black, light bulb-like form, with three white apertures transforming it into a rudimentary face or a futuristic mask and its top half enclosed in a straight edged black shape resembling Darth Vader's helmet – seems to acknowledge this in its prophetic title. While Burki's single-word titles suggest an interpretation – although highly abstracted *Augur* does resemble a soothsayer or shaman – how, or even whether, the image relates to its title is never entirely clear. Meaning emerges not as singular and bounded but as always plural, better understood as a series of tentative prognostications conjectured from signs and omens. To wit, in *Hope* (2009), the loop of black rope crisscrossing between a pair of pale grey wings – possibly angelic – is both a tether keeping the wings together and earthbound and a harness allowing one to put them on and escape, suggesting that as an ideal, utopian fantasy promises liberation but needs to be kept in check.

For Burki, an image is never an end in itself but always an illustration – of an idea or concept, of a narrative or story – and these icons distil complex narratives into single images. Despite his attempts to evacuate all vestiges of the illusory depth and narrative suggestion seen in earlier work, the barest outside reference and recognisable content still persists. Intimations of violence and sex, death and pleasure, the body and the bodily, more explicit in earlier works, are introduced in these images through the subtlest of formal tweaks. In *Watcher* (2010), a black circle, hovering above a many-sided vertical black shape floating in a field of dull blue, is transformed into an ominous omnipresent surveillance apparatus through the inclusion of a small, eye-like white aperture at its centre. *Plenitude* (2010), a grey horseshoe – a common good luck charm – with undulating edges and its open end ominously facing downwards, resembles the truncated cylinder of a revolver; the five black circles enclosed serve as individual bullet chambers. Similarly, *Source* (2009, page 121), a provocative black biomorph, whose vertical ink blot-like form appears at once both incidental and carefully engineered, is both a vaginal void topped with a trinity of breast-like bumps and an inverted phallus. And in *Lullaby* (2010), a pimple-like taupe mound, a delicately drawn black tuft lining the swelling's surface, tops a long spike. The delicious wisps resemble both hair and grass, and Burki's amusing composite oscillates between body and landscape, suggesting a possible melding of the two, with the figure and ground of traditional painting united in the understated elegance of an abstracted icon. Always playful, at times menacing, these symbols are harvested from a personal mythology of the present, at once disconcertingly familiar and completely novel.

In contrast, Burki's most recent work seems more intuitive. Though still largely frontal and dominated by a single central image, the introduction of neon colour and pattern gives these works a hallucinatory quality; like much psychedelia they seem to teeter between being truly visionary and merely kitsch. Burki's sensitivity to the specific qualities of medium used is clearly evident in a work like *Urn* (2012). A head, constructed out of variously shaded grey triangles and reminiscent of those found on Easter Island, sits at the centre of a vessel whose surface consists of interlocking triangles, each a neon rainbow of parallel lines. Black ovals distributed across this form disrupt the trippy Op-art pattern. While the translucent ink of the neon markers soaks back into the picture plane, the ovals assert its flat surface, and the sharp edges and vertices of

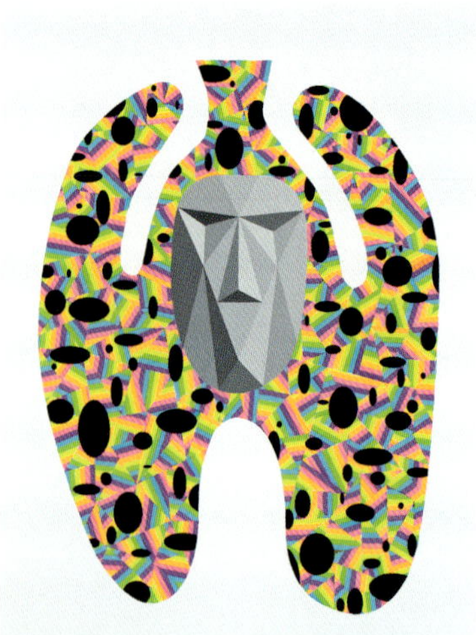

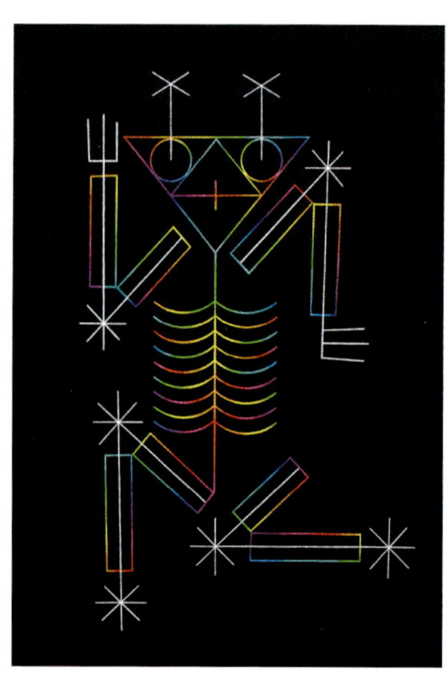

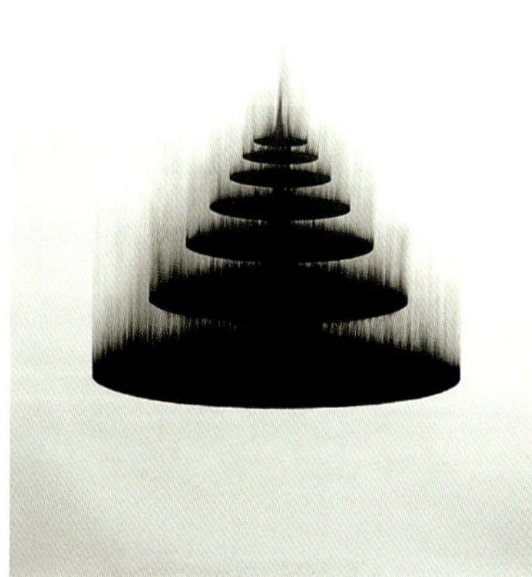

Top
Urn, 2012

Bottom left
*Stars at Elbow
and Foot*, 2012

Bottom right
Combustion 1, 2009

the head protrude ever so slightly, like bas-relief, creating a subtle but sophisticated play of flatness and depth, of form and pattern, across the composition. In other works, diagrams – where line dominates shape – are constructed out of sets of white and coloured lines etched into or scraped out of a deep black ground. The dancing stick figure in *Stars at Elbow and Foot* (2012) resembles the famous geoglyphs carved into the Nazca Desert in Southern Peru, ancient markings thought to hold astrological, cosmic or otherworldly secrets. A similarly unlikely conflation of the archaic and the futuristic, magic and technology, and spirit and science, appears in related works like *Prayer for Circuits* (2012, page 165) and *Ascent* (2012, page 167). In the former, the syntax of circuit diagrams is used to create a blueprint for transcendence, although it remains unclear whether it would be driven by human, divine or alien power. In the latter, a diamond hovers over the apex of a tall triangle; the composition's overall upward thrust again suggests an escape into the heavens.

The spectre of death seems to haunt Burki's practice. Ghosts and apparitions, ruins and bones, and funerary rites and mourning rituals reappear across his oeuvre. In *Site* (2007, pages 70–71), an early work whose title evokes an archaeological excavation, scaffolding props up parts of a half-buried statue of a man on a horse, with his sword drawn high. In this allegory of the finality of death, Burki imagines the past not as a triumphant monument, recoverable once excavated, but as a fragile ruin; the hollow black eyes of man and animal seemingly stress its irretrievability. Even the largely abstract *Combustion 1* and *Combustion 2* (2009, page 83) were inspired by Burki's interest in cremation practices.[5] The latter shows three subatomic particles or celestial bodies on the verge of collision, their movement suggested simply by smearing part of the outer edge of each black circle. The former consists of a stack of seven black discs – diminishing in size from bottom to top, so they appear to recede into the picture plane – the top edge of each carefully smudged to suggest smoke or heat rising from smouldering embers. Burki chose to use charcoal because of its similarity to ash and makes the most of its smudginess by imbuing these minimal black forms – symbols of negation and annihilation – with the littlest bit of life.[6] In Burki's view, the impulse to transcend the fact of death by imagining rebirth or an afterlife is universal and a major catalyst for the creation of the rich mythologies and iconographies he draws from and is drawn to.[7] While melancholy does permeate much of his work, it is a condition that results not from simply mourning death but from lamenting a lost connection to ancient wisdom, a disruption caused and maintained by the processes of modernity. Eternally dislocated, Burki's uncertain icons instead acknowledge the enduring power and potential of the spiritual and the sacred, of myth, mysticism and magic. They transform mythologies into futurologies, using images of and from the past to imagine, predict or, better still, prognosticate our coming days.

Murtaza Vali

5. Fahd Burki in conversation with the author, October 2013. Other related works include *Untitled* (2009), a charcoal drawing of what appears to be a bed of nails, and *Each to Their Own* (2009), a larger than life, jet black sarcophagus, standing upright, with a curious pipe jutting out from its base.
6. Ibid.
7. Ibid.

Biography

Fahd Burki (b. 1981, Lahore) graduated from the National College of Arts, Lahore, Pakistan in 2003 and pursued a Postgraduate Diploma from Royal Academy Schools, London, UK between 2008–10. He was the recipient of John Jones Art on Paper Award 2013 at Art Dubai and was one of the selected artists from the Commonwealth countries to undertake a residency at Edinburgh Printmakers. In 2014 Burki will be exhibiting his new work at Carré d'Art, Nîmes, France and a solo show will be held at Grey Noise, Dubai, UAE.

GREYNOISE

Unit 24, Alserkal Avenue Street 8,
Exit 43, SZR Al Quoz 1, Dubai, UAE
Email: info@greynoise.org
Web: www.greynoise.org